Library of Congress Cataloging-in-Publication Data

Atkins, Betsy
Behind Boardroom Doors: Lessons of a Corporate Director
Corporate governance, boards of directors, strategy, finance, ethics, accounting

Summary: A three-time CEO and experienced corporate director shares her experiences and lessons learned on the boards of some of America's biggest, most successful, and most dysfunctional companies.

ISBN-13: 978-1939282163
ISBN-10: 1939282160
BISAC: Business & Economics / Leadership
Published by Miniver Press, LLC, McLean Virginia

First edition June 2013
Second edition February 2016
Third edition April 2017

I dedicate this to my fellow public company directors and to future aspiring public company directors to share my experience and learning in the hopes that board governance continues to be more engaged and more of an asset for all stakeholders.

Betsy Atkins

Advance praise for *Behind Boardroom Doors: Lessons of a Corporate Director*

"This book is a treasure. The ultimate mystery for students, regulators, consultants, lawyers, economists—and even putative and serving members—is what goes on in the Board of Directors. Those who try to rate boards are stymied because all they have access to is public information. Betsy Atkins' book is what we all have been looking for. It is a compilation of perspectives from the inside by a really engaging narrator and professional director. I have never had such a good insight into what directors ought to do—and, truth be told, I was a director of at least a dozen publicly companies—and the great value they can impart to an enterprise. This is a treat."
-Robert A.G. Monks, founder of Institutional Shareholder Services

"As lead independent director, Betsy Atkins was responsible for integrating seven new, French board members into our SunPower board. Under her leadership, the new directors came to understand American board oversight, as well as the right level of engagement for them to be contributors and to represent all stakeholders. Readers of Betsy's book will be treated to those same leadership lessons. A fine distillation of her writings, Behind Boardroom Doors represents the culmination of Betsy's many years of experience as a director, committee chair, and industry leader."
-Tom Werner, President and CEO, SunPower

"Betsy Atkins knows corporate governance. I've been fortunate to work with her on the boards of several public companies, and watched her solve governance problems we all hope to never encounter at others. With this book she shares the wisdom that made that possible. If you represent shareholders and want to do it well, you must read this book."
-Bob Frankenberg, Lead Director, Nuance.

"Having known Betsy for many years as a trusted advisor and board 'whisperer', we most recently co-innovated on a groundbreaking initiative at the New York Stock Exchange—FORGE (The Future of Responsibility, Governance and Ethics). Here, I was able to experience a new dimension of Betsy as we assembled and captured on film the cutting-edge experiences from leading Chairmen, CEOs and government

Cabinet members. Our journey took us from Cybersecurity to Activism and beyond. Betsy was not only able to bring a formidable network to bear, but was also able to bring her decades of hard fought experience to the table and offer unparalleled perspectives into an array of complex topics. She is truly a groundbreaking figure in the governance landscape and has earned her title as the 'Balanchine of the Boardroom'."
-Adam Sodowick, President, NYSE Governance Services

"Betsy Atkin's walks the talk as a powerful competitive asset for shareholders, providing role model application of a Board Member's Duty of Care and Duty of Loyalty. As HD Supply's first Independent Director since taking HD Supply public, Betsy plays an invaluable role bringing innovative thought leadership and creating our spring board to seize major entrepreneurial trends in digitization as we focus on taking friction out of our user experiences. As our Governance Chair Betsy's practical and agile leadership is enabled through application of rigorous processes with extreme urgency. I am thankful to Betsy for sharing her lessons and for being a tremendous mentor and partner as we harness our HD Supply Board's valuable business judgement to forward build for our future."
-Joseph J. DeAngelo, Chairman and Chief Executive Officer, HD Supply

"Betsy Atkins is the consummate board member and her breath of experience, and knowledge of corporate governance, is unparalleled. I have had the privilege of serving as a fellow director with Betsy on a couple of public company boards, and we have been through a few interesting and unique experiences, including Darden Restaurants where we were both elected in conjunction with an unprecedented shareholder vote to replace the entire board. As chair of the governance committee Betsy took Darden's worst in class ISS rating to best in class in one year, by collaborating together to lead reforms, balancing the constituencies of activists and non-activist shareholders, and partnering with management as they were going though a restructuring and spinning out a REIT, all in a compressed timeframe.

"There is a big difference between the perception and the reality of serving on a public company board. Many investors and outsiders, including prospective first-time board members and board members of small or private companies, might skeptically view board service as nothing more than attending a couple of meetings a year in return for a

hefty check. The reality of effective board service is that that it is a lot of work. Yet, successful boards are also careful not to micro-manage company management teams. This book is a primer on how to achieve the right balance and how to be effective. Having served on a board with Betsy, I can attest that she brought a wealth of relevant experience to the role which she has captured in this book. Reading it felt like sitting next to Betsy and benefitting from her "war" stories, learning important lessons from a long career of both executive leadership and board service."
-Bill Lenehan, CEO Four Corners Realty Trust

"Behind Boardroom Doors is saturated with real-life examples of good, and bad, corporate governance, and I would highly recommend Betsy's book as required reading for anyone seeking to gain insights and perspectives on how to better represent shareholders, and provide exemplary board oversight."
-Lionel Nowell, lead director, Reynolds American Inc.

Behind Boardroom Doors:
Lessons of a Corporate Director

By Betsy Atkins

Miniver Press
2017

Table of Contents

Introduction

Board meetings are generally a series of sequential snapshots of the company punctuated by moments of drama and occasional crisis. A few of the most memorable board topics I've addressed include:

- A Marketing VP's wife is a porn star with a website—do we sanction this?
- A VP, Latin America Sales, is caught trying to bribe Haiti's President, Aristide's brother- in-law—do we fire him or turn him in to the DOJ?
- A Chairman's public statements directly contradict/harm the company's interests.
- A CEO wants to self enrich at the expense of the shareholders.
- Can a company's retirement pension fund be used to buy and prop up the company's stock?
- Can a company buy their CEO's son's company?

And so on. There are always new things to learn. You can never become set in your ways or rigid in your approach, or you will not be the contributor and asset your company deserves.

The board's obligation is to oversee the company and add engaged, thoughtful judgment. There are always surprises. After 20 years of serving on public boards and having sat on close to 30, I have some pattern recognition and "scar tissue" to share. The industries I've served on include Financial Services, Technology, Pharma, Hospitality, CPG, Retail, and Manufacturing, and there are more similarities than differences. They all go through crises: as you will soon read, HealthSouth did when I chaired its board and it was raided by the FBI

1

and faced prospective criminal charges from the DOJ; Lucent did, when its revenue imploded in one year from $33B to $8B and it settled fraud allegations with the SEC. NASDAQ went through a buying binge, acquiring the Boston and Philadelphia Exchanges while I served. Vonage suffered through a hugely disappointing IPO and was sued by Verizon. SunPower faced Chinese Solar Dumping and brought in Total Oil as a controlling owner. Polycom and Chico's successfully went through a CEO succession.

As a three-time CEO and "professional director" on public and private U.S. and International companies experiencing 11 IPO's, three bankruptcies, many CEO changes, acquisitions, divestitures, "go private's" and mergers of equals, I've learned many lessons. The most valuable has been how to do "active listening," apply pattern recognition, and be ever vigilant about the competition in the marketplace. Based on my roots as a technology entrepreneur I believe companies must continuously innovate and embrace new business models and technologies as rocket fuel for differentiation, efficiency, and leadership. Every company will always be disrupted sooner than they expect. Serving on European-based boards has taught me the power of global teams.

Most boards perform well, but I've come to believe they can do better, becoming a competitive asset for the shareholders. In this book, I share my insights from this compilation of articles I've written in hopes they will be helpful for those interested in the inner workings of global boardrooms. Each article contains one or more "lessons," summarized in italics, that I hope will become a part of your personal corporate director's toolkit.

I begin with the best advice I ever gave. May this, and all these hard-won lessons, be of use as you pursue your own important work.

B.A.

These high-level tips boil down to one lesson: you must be willing to do the crisis work yourself. As directors we're responsible for business judgment. There is no substitute for doing this critical work.

The Best Advice I Ever Gave a Board

Act as if it were your own company.

Upon joining a company hit with accounting fraud to chair a special litigation committee days before insolvency and joining a telecom company board during a market meltdown, I faced two crises:

- The telecom market meltdown lesson: In restructuring, do the deepest cut first, and cut more than you think you will ever need to—it's better for the organization and the shareholders than death by 1000 razor blade cuts.
- The accounting fraud company lesson: In a crisis, you must meet daily, prioritize the most important and urgent decisions, and power through them. Everyone must be on every board call, and there can be no stalling, as decisions must be made when the company teeters into the "zone of insolvency" with no CEO and no chairman.

Do your own diligence yourself. Personally interview and find the best advisers in each category: turnaround firms, forensic accounting firms, and new law firms with depth in the specific areas needed. Insist on selecting the on-site team.

Communicate daily and openly with all constituencies: board colleagues, employees, shareholders, press, and vendors. Lastly, if you make all your decisions as if the company were your own company, community, and employees, with their best interests, to stabilize and build a business for the long term, you will have done the right thing and can sleep soundly.

Adapted from *Directors & Boards* 4th Quarter 2006.

3

CHAPTER 1: CEO SUCCESSION AND SUCCESS

Leading Your Board—To Do List for a New CEO

Set the Tone

Here are a few "rules-of-the-road" in constructing and leading your board. Boards are like any other group and they perform best when they are well led, (as contracted with "managed" death by powerpoint.)

To maximize your board's effectiveness, you need to help them by setting the right tone as CEO. First, you will be well served if you make it a part of your standard cadence to call each board member a week or so before the board meeting. These are brief 10 minute calls just to see what's on their mind as issues or topics. If there is a big concern a member has, you have the opportunity to diffuse it rather than be ambushed and subsequently napalmed in the meeting.

CEO Letter

One idea I have seen work well is to consider writing a brief 1 to 2 page letter to the board a few days before the meeting. This helps to focus the board on the key points.

State of the Union

A best practice I've seen is that the CEO starts each board meeting with a mini "state of the union" soliloquy. This has the benefit of reinforcing your role as CEO and leader, and focusing the board on the key topics of the board meeting.

"The Board eats what you serve them"

Specifically, when you don't identify a topic you are seeking input/guidance on, then the board will just jump in and can take the discussion down tangents that are less productive. Boards are made of smart, motivated people who want to make a contribution. It's incumbent on you to lead them to the right subjects.

Board members want to participate and contribute. The best way to engage your board and to get value out of their experience is to identify the strategic subjects (1-3) where you specifically seek their input. For example, you might raise a significant topic like: "when and where we should expand to new international geographies?" or a fork in a product road map decision. In each example, you ought to have a management recommendation and seek the board's input.

Each director should take the Hippocratic Oath: "Do no harm to the patient"

The board's role is oversight, not overstep. New board members sometimes have a learning curve on this. Your Chairman or Lead independent director should help guide new board members on the correct level of engagement... what's helpful... what's not. You will do well if you give the feedback to your Chair or Lead on directors who are drifting from oversight to overstep. Do this early if you experience this.

Just as the board will discuss you, your team, and the company's status in the executive session, you also should share any feedback on the board's performance to your Lead/Chair.

A satisfying and productive board meeting will cover 2-3 big strategic topics. The board's package with last quarter's financial performance and the forward looking financial targets for the remainder of the year should be sent to the board 3 days prior the meeting at a minimum. Expect and assume your board has read these materials and thought about them. You will irritate the board if you waste 25 percent of the board meeting reciting this information. Be prepared to present the key financial insights on growth, costs, profit, sharing your analysis about the concerns and conclusions on the numbers.

Choosing your Board Members

Building your board is a key and crucial job where you want to be both thoughtful and maybe a bit paranoid. Your board should be a true

5

competitive asset for your company. Standard committee oversight and competence are table stakes. You should plan over time that you may evolve and forward hire (or do board renewal) just as you do with your direct reports.

To enable "board renewal," I recommend you put into your governance principles that the role of the Lead Director or Chairman auto-sunsets each year. A typical term for a Lead/Chair is often 5-7 years, however, if you were to get sideways and out of alignment with this key board leader, you need a mechanism that enables you to remedy this.

Along the lines of "a little paranoid" here are a few tips: Your longevity in the role of the CEO directly correlates to your personal engagement in selecting your directors. If you don't ensure that within the first 18 months or so you have had a high level of involvement in selecting at least 1/3 of your directors, statistically your term will be less than 5 years.

Skills Matrix
Sometimes you need a technique to "rotate-off" your board members. They might be investors or simply directors you have outgrown. A non-emotional, face-saving method is to create together with the board a collective view of the skills/expertise/perspective needed to be an asset for the corporations coming five years. So for example, your skills matrix might include: deep domain knowledge, experience in scaling through hyergrowth; global go-to-market, M&A and post merger integration, financial expert, Compensation Committee Chair experience etc.

Diversity of Thought
Diversity of thought is very valuable to board discussions, sometimes people characterize this as gender or race diversity. While this is part of the concept, I would posit that bringing directors from different geographies, or maybe a customer perspective, or an adjacent industry perspective enriches discussion and constructively helps stress test logic and ideas.

Beware and Be Aware
Additionally, a horrifying statistic is that 25 percent of CEO terminations are replaced by board members. There was no succession plan. What's most disturbing is that anecdotally after serving on ~25 public boards, I believe maybe half of those 25 percent were coup d'états... assassinations. Don't invite Machiavelli into your board room.

Ask for Help and Follow Up

During your board meetings directors, often offer introductions/help leveraging their networks…(as they should); these offers are almost never followed up on. Ask your Lead Director or Chair to capture these offers for follow up/follow through. Additionally, often there is an important request by a director to get further information on a subject or for a follow-up discussion on a question raised. Create a mechanism in your board meetings to capture these requests or you will frustrate and annoy your board and seem unresponsive.

Exec Session

The Executive Session is a standard ISS and SEC prescribed best practice. Exec sessions are the time when the directors meet without the CEO, led by the Chairman or the Lead Director. Every board meeting should have an Exec Session. The directors will typically review the board meeting that's just concluded, discuss their impressions of the CEO and leadership team, as well as the company's performance. They tend to focus on areas of opportunity, challenge, or concern. They serve to keep the directors aligned. It's key the Chair/Lead be a good facilitator to capture each members views and importantly helps head off any runaway tangents.

A good Chair/Lead will solicit and capture views from each director then do a roll up summary with the board. The next step is the read out to the CEO. Many approaches work—the CEO can join the directors and receive the summary with all directors present, or more often the Chair/Lead alone or with one other director present (often a committee chair) will meet alone with the CEO to share the read out of the executive session. The CEO may want to take notes here and be sure that all the feedback is captured and identified for follow ups. This should always be a constructive and helpful session.

In conclusionm your board is there to perform its fiduciary duty as stewards for the shareholders, but more importantly to help coach, mentor and maximize the CEO and the company's potential for the long term. Select your board wisely and run your meetings well and they will be an accelerant for your business!

Adapted from *Corporate Board Member Magazine* 2Q 2016.

7

Be sure the board has a unified view of the leadership characteristics they want in a new CEO, and how much change is desired. Often the most important characteristics are qualitative.

The Most Important Role of the Board

The most important responsibility of the board of directors is to hire the CEO (and then measure his or her performance). When hiring a CEO, it is very important that the board, through discussion, build consensus on the specifications being sought—the quantitative measurable characteristics and, more importantly, the qualitative soft characteristics.

Oftentimes it is easy to select a CEO based on quantitative measurable performance, such as evidence of stock price increase, or specific background experience, such as technical background, merger experience, or marketing know-how. These are things that can be measured. But the attributes that impact success in corporate leadership are often the softer qualitative attributes. You need to be able to assess a candidate's vision, their ability to inspire, their passion and their convictions, and, most importantly, their leadership.

Leadership is something that is difficult to define. Leadership is often a collection of personal behaviors, political skills, and people skills that enable the leader to get people to follow. In order to inspire people to follow you, you have to demonstrate to your prospective followers that they can trust and believe in you, that the values that you communicate are ones that they can and should believe in, and that you have integrity. In order to be successful, you also need to have the ability to empathize with your team. An example would be AT&T's Mike Armstrong: His direct reports will tell you that he truly cares about them, that he makes them feel included, and that he is empathetic, so it is a natural thing to follow him.

A leader has to be able to see the big picture and not get lost in the details. It is also important for the leader to have had multifunctional responsibilities—so that, for example, you are not recruiting for a chief executive a CFO who is shifting for the first time from being a single functional leader to what is a multi-function general manager role.

It is very important that the board have a shared view of leadership and the importance of this attribute. Sometimes there is not total agreement on the board about how much change the board re- ally wants. It is important that there be consensus on the board because leaders, being agents of change, may be threatening.

Leadership is a destabilizing attribute—creating a vision, building consensus, motivating people to make changes for the growth of the company. Sometimes people resist true leadership because they feel threatened and do not want to shake anything up.

Most companies do not have a good track record at developing internal leadership. Although statistics show that more than 65% of CEOs were the No. 2 before getting the top job, the No. 2 person is not always the best leader. In fact, most No. 2s have not been successful when becoming the CEO. Coca-Cola's appointment of Douglas Ivester is one example among many recent cases.

It is very important when using an outside headhunter that the board gives a uniform view of what they want in terms of quantitative skills as well as qualitative leadership attributes.

Some questions that are helpful to ask when trying to measure the "soft" characteristics of leadership are:

- Has the candidate demonstrated the ability to lead and develop talent?
- Can this perceptive leader energize others?
- Are they comfortable delegating power to other people?
- Does this leader hold his or her team accountable for delivering on promises and specific performance?
- Does this person inspire people to follow and trust them and do they really listen to others in a respectful way?
- Does this leader share information, resources, praise, and credit?

It is important to note that people who interview well for CEO may not be the right person. Oftentimes someone who has great charisma has a big ego, and that does not necessarily make a great CEO. An effective leader gets things done through other people. They have to be able to get everybody focused on their vision of the company's strategic direction and to galvanize the whole organization for a positive change.

Selecting the CEO is the most important decision that the board will make. The next key item is to be sure that there is a compensation structure that supports the objectives of the corporation and allows the board to measure and reward the CEO for achieving these goals.

Great CEOs are hard to find and hire, but succession is the board's most important role.

Adapted from *Directors and Boards* Summer 2001.

All CEO candidates should have strong track records. Be sure to interview potential CEOs in informal and social settings to listen for softer leadership attributes of team building and credit sharing. Do some of the background checks yourself to hear the important nuances of how the candidate is described.

What to Look for When Hiring a CEO

The most critical skills are the ones you can't quantify.

As a three-time CEO and now director on a number of boards, I can attest that directors have learned a lot in recent years about hiring chief executives. For one thing, they're trying harder to promote from within, rather than hiring charismatic but untested CEOs from the outside. But sometimes an external search is necessary, and boards have to try to build a consensus on the specifications being sought. While there are many quantitative measurements, such as stock price history or background experience, the attributes that may have the greatest impact on a candidate's potential success are softer, qualitative ones. That's why directors need to be able to assess a candidate's passion and strength of convictions, as well as his or her ability to lead.

I should acknowledge that I am by no means perfect in this regard. Case in point: I sat briefly on the HealthSouth board. Although CEO Richard Scrushy was impressive and forceful, there was something about him that raised my antennae but I never pinpointed what it was. I now understand that the charismatic "star" CEO leadership style is inconsistent with developing an open environment and an empowered management team. We did a better job of paying attention to the softer skills at Lucent Technologies, where I was also a board member, when we decided to recruit Pat Russo. Knowing that Lucent was going through significant upheaval and needed a high-integrity, inspiring team builder to stabilize and rebuild, we emphasized those soft values of leadership. And that's what they have now in Russo, as CEO.

Wiser for these experiences, I'm convinced that one absolute key in assessing a candidate is the social interaction that directors have with him or her. It's a mistake to hire a CEO solely on the basis of formal presentations and discussions. After all, leadership is a collection of personal behaviors, political and people skills, and judgment—and much of that is typically suppressed in formal settings.

In social interactions, it's easier to ask open-ended questions such as, what are you proudest of in your career? Or what was the most difficult challenge you ever faced? A director with a well-trained ear can then discover whether the candidate thinks in terms of building teams to accomplish objectives or is a lone ranger.

I also think it is crucial for directors to conduct some background checks themselves, rather than relying entirely on others. These sorts of conversations often produce new insight into a candidate's personality. You can hear the nuances in pregnant pauses that aren't always apparent in a preference write-up. It's not that I don't trust the executive search firms that typically handle this work. It's just that they obviously have an incentive to close the transaction through a hiring decision, rather than prolong the debate.

By having both formal and informal contact with a candidate and being directly involved in checking references, directors stand a much better chance of understanding the skills he or she offers. Consider what leadership means: To inspire people to follow you, you have to demonstrate they can trust and believe in you, that the values you communicate are ones they can and should believe in, and that you have integrity and judgment. There's no way to analyze those qualities on a spreadsheet.

Here are some questions to consider when measuring these "softer" characteristics:

- Has the candidate demonstrated the ability to lead and develop talent?
- Can this leader energize others? Is he or she comfortable delegating power?
- Does this leader hold his or her team accountable for delivering on promises and specific performance?
- Does this leader share information, resources, praise and credit?

Going into a search, the board must have a shared view of leadership, and directors must agree on how much change they want; a search can be crippled from the start if some directors fear the new leader will change things too drastically. But if directors can agree, and if they are sensitive to the softer attributes, they can make a decision that will benefit the company for years to come.

Adapted from *Chief Executive Magazine* May 2004.

There is often a disconnect between pay for short-term company performance and the long-term needs of institutional investors for intrinsic enterprise value. One thing compensation committees can do is to be sure they are paying for business performance as opposed to stock market performance. A key is to be sure CEO and top management pay is designed to differentiate between short-term, operational work and long-term, strategic work.

Pay for Long Term

Compensation committees face a fundamental problem: Executive pay has been based on short-term performance, but institutional investors require long-term results. The disconnect is that short-term company performance is being rewarded with pay for long term. Many boards and institutional investors are asking, "How much?" rather than the more important question, "For what results?" There are big gaps between executive accountability and the measures of longer-term performance, such as "intrinsic enterprise value" in the marketplace. We should all be in favor of equitable compensation, but concerned about excessive compensation.

The big problem in companies today is that often CEOs and senior executives are held accountable for short-term (one to two year) operational work, yet they are paid as if they are accountable for longer-term (three to five year) strategic work and value creation. Boards often don't identify the right goals and metrics for the longer time frames necessary to effectively measure CEO performance. We need to motivate and reward leaders to create longer-term enterprise and shareholder value.

Executive compensation needs to include pay for performance. Specifically, what performance should be measured is the key question. Data reported in a New York Stock Exchange report shows that the majority of executives were held to too low a level of accountability. In that report, a financial analysis of the top 800 public companies (approximately 85 percent of the U.S. market), showed that, over the five years ending in 2003, 60 percent failed to pro- vide a net operating profit after tax greater than their cost of capital. This low return on invested capital makes one ask, "How viable are the business models of these companies?" What exactly are boards holding those CEOs accountable for? This is a key test to measure board effectiveness.

Compensation policies in proxies showed 90 percent of the S&P 500 CEOs and their executive teams were not held accountable—or paid—for business performance (as opposed to stock market performance) beyond two years. The difficulty is that shareholders, especially institutional investors/ pension funds, are accountable for long-term liabilities and only a few companies have begun to make the longer-term compensation changes needed.

CEO compensation has increased from 40 times that of the average worker in 1982 to more than 500 times in 2000. Many options are still granted without setting any type of multi-year performance targets. We can more closely align stock options with shareholder benefits by predicating their vesting on meeting multi-year performance targets.

In setting accountabilities, boards need to look at the top two or three levels of management to be sure CEO goals and objectives are consistent with the rest of the senior team's compensation goals and metrics. It's important to set goals across multiple levels for the long-term measure, not just a short- term, one-to-two-year time frame.

Some topics for directors to think about when setting pay:

1. Create a process and document it; courts will ask in the future whether one was used. Have detailed committee minutes with management attachments showing there is pay for measurable performance.
2. Show that decisions were made in good faith (see Disney). Directors need to be able to show that they exercised good faith in order to rely on the business judgment rule, including documenting their efforts to be objectively informed using outside studies and advisors.
3. Ensure that the CEO pay plan is designed to differentiate short-term operational work from long- term strategic work.
4. Create a measurable set of milestones that pay out only if achieved.
5. Detail strategic deliverables and three- to five-year metrics for the CEO and executives to create long-term sustainable value for all stakeholders.

15

Betsy Atkins

6. Ensure that total executive compensation is equitable based on objective comparisons.

Companies that have set only one- to two-year short-term operational targets for EBITDA (earnings before interest, taxes, depreciation, and amortization), earnings, and earnings per share from current operations may have set the goal too low. Today only 11 percent of the S&P 500 have disclosed a time period beyond three years for measuring business performance, as opposed to stock market performance. Three-to-five-year return on invested capital may be a better measure to analyze whether management is creating real value.

Compensation committees will need to be more rigorous going forward. Only through informed decisions about accountability, and what they are paying for, can boards and CEOs carry out their fiduciary duties and defend their decisions on what they pay. Doing this will strengthen the link between pay and performance, and ultimately create value for the company and its shareholders.

Adapted from *Directors Monthly* July 2005.

Machiavelli in the Boardroom

It may not be stilettos and poison rings, but new CEO/princes face real boardroom dangers.

In my career as a company founder, venture capitalist, and corporate director, I've met many business leaders, thinkers and doers. All have offered good advice on launching, managing and monitoring an enterprise. But many of these leaders are a bit shy on sharing insights on a tricky, but important, aspect of leadership—how the savvy chief executive manages his or her board of directors. So, I thought I'd check in with one particular longtime acquaintance on high-stakes career management in the real world. Niccolò Machiavelli, 15th century Italian diplomat, courtier, and author of *The Prince*, thoughtfully answered my email (on parchment, no less) on how our modern boardroom princes should use *realpolitik* to survive and thrive.

"Thank you for your query, Betsy, and for the information you thoughtfully included. If the longevity of CEO positions today has truly declined to 4.5 years, it would seem that the overthrow of sovereigns now is even more common than in the time of the Medicis (albeit less deadly).

There seem to be various factors in making the modern chief executive short lived. The most frequent cause of CEO turnover is company underperformance relative to peers (though there seem to be many exceptions to this rule). The board of directors then may lose confidence in the prince, particularly if shareholders are raising a din outside the castle gates.

However, the board of directors of the enterprise may bring less democratic impulses to their governance role. CEOs of companies which feature a separate board chair, particularly a founder or emeritus chairman, are especially vulnerable. This powerful, independent boardroom leader's views carry great weight with the other directors, and he can be mercurial in his support or opposition to the chief. Though a founder may have been the incoming CEO's sponsor or mentor, he can prove fickle if the founding legacy seems at risk, and do a turnabout to lead a boardroom rebellion.

While the founder or emeritus chair may claim the highest of motives for such a revolt, we often find the replacement CEO to be none other than *the founder or emeritus chair himself.* Indeed, it is quite possible that *any* of the princelings gathered around that board table may in fact be seeking your crown. The ideal director is a current or recent CEO with fresh experience, mentoring ability, and the perspective of a business leader who's 'been there, done that,' in the current phrase. This makes them estimable board members—and likewise ideal "interim" CEOs. Recent figures show that about one-fifth of U.S. CEO turnover finds the job taken by a current board member. Novice CEOs, in particular, may face directors who are not thinking 'How can I help this CEO do a better job?' but rather *'I* should be the one doing this job!'

Thus, the new CEO/prince faces real boardroom dangers. However, there are a few tactics he or she should exercise that will help. First is to announce that you'd like to 'refresh' and 'renew' the board to make it a stronger partner in governance. Encourage board evaluation and director succession planning—which, of course, will lead to some board turnover. Even two or three new board members can help reshape the board's perspective and better align it with your own vision. Of course, it will not harm your cause if these new members not only share your strategic goals but are allies.

Board renewal and best practices should shift membership in other ways. Even if a founder or emeritus chair is your current supporter, governance 'best practice' seeks to retire such veterans from the board. Done right, the board will seek the good governance benefits of the founder's retirement—and relieve you of a potential threat.

I should note, however, that the modern board of directors, particularly those of public companies, no longer accepts their past status as lapdogs for a powerful chief executive. Poor performance will lead any board today toward rebelliousness. My era offered the handy leadership tools of the Borgias to enforce discipline—stilettos and poison rings. CEOs now must survive through less exciting measures, such as solid EPS and share price. However, that should *not* mean ignoring political boardroom realities that can help improve his odds."

Adapted from *Directors & Boards Magazine* Q2 2014

CHAPTER 2: CRISIS MANAGEMENT

Major board crises are infrequent; however, every director eventually faces a big issue. The key is to create and follow a "pristine process." Don't panic, just remember as a public company director you have two key duties:

1. *Duty of care: If you are careful, thoughtful, and thorough in getting objective information as a basis for your decision, any decision you make will be protected under the business judgment rule.*
2. *Duty of loyalty: You must ensure that your decision is based on what is best for the shareholders and the long-term health of the enterprise, and that there are no conflicts of interest. In other words, no director personally benefits from the decision.*

My 16 Days on the HealthSouth Board

It's every director's nightmare: joining the board of a company just before it is hit by charges of massive criminal fraud, that's what happened to Betsy Atkins last March. (Ed. Note: March 2003)

In this exclusive account—based on a diary she kept as events unfolded, e-mails she exchanged with other directors, and interviews with *Corporate Board Member*'s Colin Leinster—Atkins reconstructs what the board discussed the day the FBI moved in, what she did to help the company stay in business, how she put together the professional backup the board needed in its time of crisis, and why she suddenly decided to RESIGN.

The allegations came right out of the blue. The SEC hadn't requested any information or data before filing its complaint, which I think it usually does in such cases. It had certainly done so before announcing its investigation into insider trading, and these new allegations were clearly very much more serious. We weren't just looking at manageable fines here; if anyone were to prove criminal fraud against the company, HealthSouth could be out of business.

As chair of the special litigation committee, I knew that the board had to make a series of immediate decisions to try and minimize the damage. And as the newest member of the board, and therefore the most objective, I took it upon myself to chair an emergency board meeting later that day, something we could do via a conference call.

I started to keep a diary of what I did and of what the board needed to do, sometimes making handwritten notes, sometimes dictating them. I see that I began March 19's entry with a typo, saying it "started as a regularly day." Then I noted that after I got word of the criminal allegations, I went to my computer to call up the Associated Press article, and printed it. "From there," I wrote, "Things cascaded at a rapid pace." I listed some of the events of that day, breaking them down by the hour:

By 10:00 am EST, I had received phone calls from 5 of the board members.

By 11:00 am, I was on a telephone conference call, the first impromptu board meeting of the day with [board members] Sage Givens, Chuck Newhall, and George Strong.

By 12:00 noon, I had spoken to Joel Gordon, the largest shareholder and [a] board member who sold his surgery centers to HealthSouth.

By 1:00 pm I was on a Special Investigation Committee call with Wilson Sonsini's Bruce Vanyo [the lawyer I'd picked to represent the committee] discussing the SEC complaint, analyzing it, reviewing it, and determining the impact of this complaint.

By 5:00 pm EST, there was a board call of the entire board including Mr. Scrushy.

This last entry isn't quite accurate. One director, Bob May, was on a cruise and we couldn't get through to him in time. Jon Hanson was on a plane. He got through, but the static was so bad he drowned us all out and had to hang up. In addition, Bill Horton, HealthSouth's corporate lawyer, joined the conference call, as did a large number of other lawyers representing all kinds of interested parties, including HealthSouth itself, Mr. Scrushy, William Owens, the CFO, different individual directors, and various board committees, including my own. Even the corporate counsel had his counsel on the line. They all kept jumping in, and it was often impossible to know who was speaking for whom.

The one clear decision we made that afternoon was that the board would cooperate fully in the Justice Department's investigation. It was agreed I'd chair and host daily emergency board meetings for the foreseeable future. It was clear I would be very busy. As it was, I have six lines at my office in Coral Gables, and all of them were lit up from six in the morning until 11 at night from that point on.

At 7:30 p.m. that same day we had another board meeting, this one with just the outside directors. In other words, we met without the CEO or CFO being present.

Looking back over several pages of handwritten notes about what we needed to discuss at our second emergency board meeting that day, I see that I referred to one concern over and over, using different words to do so. Perhaps I got closest to the point when I wrote:

First thing to worry about is who drives the bus.

I stated this somewhat more officially in an e-mail I had sent the other board members by way of an agenda that outlined what I thought we needed to discuss when we met again at 7:30. I prioritized a number of issues, the top three being:

1. Should we remove Mr. Scrushy and put him on administrative leave?
2. Who would become the chairman?
3. Who would become the CEO?

We also needed to decide the future of our CFO, I said, because of the new allegations. We would have to decide whether to put them both on administrative leave or terminate them. To terminate Scrushy would trigger his $15 million severance contract, however, because he hadn't been convicted of anything.

So at our meeting that night, we voted to put Mr. Scrushy on administrative leave rather than fire him. We made the same decision regarding Mr. Owens. Both had to leave the building, and neither was to be allowed back in, let alone anywhere near the computers. We also voted to bar them from company planes. The risk of their taking flight was something we had to consider.

Finding somebody to serve as chairman and CEO was clearly the issue on everybody's mind, and took up a lot of our discussion. In the end, we decided to split the jobs. Joel Gordon agreed to be chairman, and he was a good choice. He was the biggest individual shareholder, after all, and was familiar with the health-care business. For CEO, we zeroed in on Bob May, who agreed to take the job on an acting basis.

The meeting lasted until 9:30, and by the time we hung up we had put together a press release that laid out the big changes at the top of the company. This demonstrated to outsiders, including the Justice Department, that the board was taking the crisis seriously. We said nothing about a replacement CFO; that was something we had yet to decide on. The release also identified the various directors who'd signed on to different committees.

I was careful to write down all the other things we never got around to but needed to discuss fast. As I noted after that meeting:

We need to do a lot of things in a short period of time.

I had known before I even joined the board that HealthSouth had legal problems, albeit relatively minor ones compared with what we now faced. In fact, that's why I'd been recruited in the first place. About six months previously, the SEC had begun an investigation of insider trading by Mr. Scrushy—specifically, that he knew Medicare was dropping reimbursement levels for various treatments and had unloaded some of his stock before the cutbacks became public knowledge and hurt the price of HealthSouth shares. The company was determined to face up to whatever lay ahead and wanted to find a new director who could also serve as the chair of the special litigation committee and help it through its legal issues. I seemed to fit the role because I had experience as a director of a number of companies, including Lucent Technologies that had faced other legal difficulties.

The way I was recruited was an elaborate and highly transparent process—a very good example of the "best practices." The recruiting firm, the screening committee, and the members of the nominating committee all made the same pitch, telling me that HealthSouth was a stable, profitable, high-growth outfit and the leader in its business sector.

Everybody I interviewed with tried to prepare me for Richard Scrushy. In particular, I was told about his strong and flamboyant "big" personality. I assured the nominating committee that I'd encountered several high-ego founders in my past, since I come out of the technology industry, where such characters are not unusual.

The job looked interesting and challenging. I had no doubts about HealthSouth's own state of health. Its approach to high-quality patient service, coupled with an integrated model of diagnostic facilities, surgery centers, and rehab centers, was unique, and the industry itself, of course, is a high-growth one.

I decided to accept HealthSouth's offer because I believed in the value and promise of its business. The opportunity to chair the special litigation committee was intellectually challenging and complex. It was obvious that I'd be signing up for a very significant amount of work, however, and I accordingly decided not to stand for reelection on two other boards. That way I would be able to dedicate all the time that I knew HealthSouth would need. I looked forward to the future.

I dove right into my new job. One of the first tasks I set myself was to take a hard look at all the dozen or so law firms that the company was paying—nationally known ones and what seemed to be a lot of local firms in Birmingham. Some of them, national and local, were billing like crazy. From the very start I had realized that the special litigation committee, of which I was the only member, would need its own legal counsel. I also realized that some of my fellow board members were perhaps overly influenced by Richard Scrushy. He'd handpicked them, after all.

In fact, Scrushy tried to turn his charm on me once I'd joined the board, probably to see how he might influence how I'd approach the insider-trading allegations. He called me at home on a couple of occasions to try to volunteer his version of history. But my conversations with him were very limited. I had the responsibility to investigate him, after all, and I did not want to taint my committee's independence. Remember, its predecessor had been condemned by the Delaware Court for just that reason. The committee had hired its own independent attorney, and I wanted him present when we interviewed Mr. Scrushy.

As things turned out, we never did have that meeting. The events of March 19 more or less took care of that.

March 20 wasn't any calmer. I spent the morning either at my computer or on the phone, much of it talking with or about professionals who could provide financial advice and crisis management. The board needed both, fast.

Over the course of the day, I sent a series of e-mails to the board members that underscored this conviction, faxing copies to George Strong, who didn't do e-mail. Here are some excerpts:

9:47 a.m. to Chuck Newhall et al.:

One of the first things the Special Investigation Committee needs to do is to hire a forensic accounting firm to immediately start to determine the status of the company's financials. I have identified the leading forensic investigator practitioners from PricewaterhouseCoopers, KPMG and Deloitte & Touche. I have calls in to all 3 and completed my first interview with [the] PricewaterhouseCoopers practice leader who has just completed the WorldCom, Adelphia and Xerox investigations. I've obtained a quotation range and confirmed his immediate availability.

I have asked PricewaterhouseCoopers to put out on their internal high level partner email list a request if they can identify any outstanding public company CFO candidates that could go in on an acting basis. Mike Kelly of the Directorship Search Group is also trying to identify high caliber proven credible public company CFOs who could go in on an acting basis.

Joel mentioned a previous long-time colleague he felt could step in, but I thought we ought to have some back up sources in case for some reason his colleague is unable to immediately step in to assist.

Just before noon, I heard from Joel Gordon and George Strong. They raised the issue of whether HealthSouth could stay solvent. I passed that concern on to the rest of the board, along with thoughts I had on that subject:

I think we may need to understand if we have free and clear assets that we can pledge, as well as obtain an adequate credit line to be able to go through a restructuring/refinancing. We're working on this with CS First Boston.

I used that same e-mail to repeat my belief that we needed to get a restatement/re-audit—and that we needed to look at the ramifications of taking the company into Chapter 11.

I think it's essential to contact E&Y [Ernst & Young, the company's auditor] both in Birmingham and at their most senior level to get a commitment from them (if they will agree) to commence a re-audit. I will be investigating names of the most experienced financial advisory firms, i.e., Lazard was used at Adelphia. I'll find out who WorldCom used.

A key issue the board needs to be informed and decide on very shortly will be the trade-offs and issues associated with potentially going into bankruptcy. I will be pulling together a briefing on this for us so we can be informed and be able to make a thoughtful decision in a timely manner.

The SEC had suspended trading in HealthSouth, a ban that was to last four days—a record. But the stock was sure to take a big hit, and I worried that a good company might suddenly be very vulnerable. In other words, we needed to look not only at whether the company might end up insolvent—and at what that would mean to the directors personally—but also at whether we should set an entire meeting aside to discuss how to handle any unsolicited takeover bids.

25

I see that in the summary of notes I made to myself at this time that listed all the things I had to do, I wrote a short and perhaps desperate:

I need to get someone else on the Cmte with me.

Another e-mail I put together over the morning of the 20th contained my recommendation that the board hire two forms of specialized help, a crisis-management firm and one that could act as a financial adviser. I gave my reasoning:

In a serious situation where our liquidity and solvency is uncertain, we as a board need to engage the appropriate adviser team. Crisis managers have been used at Enron, WorldCom, etc. They are operating people who augment our Chairman and CEO. Their role is to run the business day to day and address near term liquidity issues and keep the company from hemorrhaging and melting down. They provide the financial institutions with comfort that someone untainted is there to protect their interest and help restore credibility. Financial advisers address the liquidity question and how to go about satisfying our liquidity needs. Financial advisers facilitate the access to capital and work with our lenders and bondholders as well as address the accuracy of reliable financial projects. [I supplied the names of both kinds of outfits, financial advisory firms and crisis-management firms, along with their phone numbers, so that my fellow board members could do whatever further checking they cared to do.]

Please think about the recommendation I have, which is we engage immediately a crisis management firm and a financial advisory firm. I would like your views on this.

I had also spoken with Harvey Kelly, a leader in the forensic accounting investigative practice at PricewaterhouseCoopers, and recommended that the board hire him as well. I passed along what he had to say about the conventional wisdom/best practice approach in a situation like ours, and gave the board his recommendation for the two best crisis-management firms.

Later I got back to the board with what I'd found out about the ability of KPMG to act as our forensic accountants. I'd asked KPMG the same questions I'd asked Pricewaterhouse, including "Should we retain a crisis-management firm to help manage the creditors?" (They said yes and offered some suggestions.) They said they were conflicted about recommending a financial adviser, because they wanted that work themselves. I used the same e-mail to urge the board to reach three important decisions at the 2 p.m. board meeting that now lay only an hour away.

Board Decisions

1. We should review and hopefully approve the retention of a forensic accounting organization in today's board meeting.
2. We should review and hopefully approve a financial advisory firm.
3. We should review and hopefully approve a crisis management firm.

With two minutes to go before the board meeting, I sent another e-mail. It began and ended with a recommendation that I really hoped they'd go for:

May I suggest that for the first hour of the phone call, we have no attorneys on the call so we can sort out the key issues:

1. Liquidity—Specifically George can give us an update with E&Y regarding a re-audit on a potential credit line from CSFB.
2. Solvency Issues—Create a plan to determine if we can remain solvent and get counsel from Weil Gotshal.
3. Legal Issues—There are too many law firms. Our legal issues fall into 3 major categories:
   a. Investigative: Betsy to select.
   b. Insolvency/Restructuring Questions: The board to select. Weil Gotshal is the nation's leading firm and seems ready to jump in.
   c. Regulatory/SEC/Criminal/Civil Shareholder derivatives lawsuit: Here the criminal potential of RICO claims against the company could put us out of business.

Please let me know if you think this is the appropriate agenda. Do you have other suggested topics we should add to the agenda? Do you agree we should discourage having a wide range of attorneys dialing into this call? I believe it is not advisable at this juncture to have so many outside attorneys. Bill Horton will not be on this call. I'm anxious to hear your thoughts.

Obviously I wasn't the only one who wanted to cut back on the number of lawyers, because there were only two on the line for our next meeting: Bruce Vanyo and Michael Young of Willkie Farr & Gallagher, representing the audit committee. Even then it was a long meeting, but by the end of it we had selected Kelly and his PWC team to do our forensic accounting. The board also agreed on the need for a crisis-management firm. Joel Gordon and Bob May, in their new roles, agreed to interview the two finalists for the work the following day. Gordon agreed to take a company plane from his home in Nashville to Birmingham—a very necessary presence. The whole board was working very hard.

Even before that meeting had begun, I was putting together another agenda for our meeting the following day, the 21st. This primarily addressed the company's need for strong legal representation. I'd already done considerable homework on what we should be looking for, and outlined the characteristics I and the lawyers I'd consulted thought such firms should have:

1. SEC experience
2. The ability to manage massive sets of litigations, and derivative and shareholder lawsuits
3. Knowledge of insolvency and bankruptcy
4. Experience with public company securities law
5. Employment law experience.

The attorneys I'd spoken to recommended two firms in particular that met these requirements. They agreed, too, on which firms had to go—a group that included many of the Birmingham outfits.

Overview
In thinking about the counsel issue, I divide our legal needs into three "baskets": (i) general corporate and insolvency counsel, to assist the board on a going-forward basis as it considers the general business and fiduciary issues facing us over the near term; (ii) regulatory counsel, to respond to the inquiries and investigations from the SEC and U.S.

Attorney's offices and possibly other governmental agencies; and (iii) counsel to investigate and issue a report on the allegations of past misconduct.

It is my inclination to get new counsel for all of these roles. I am concerned about the appearance of conflict that any of our prior counsel may have, as well as the possibility that actual conflicts exist. In addition, I am of the view that the gravity of our situation demands that we have the best possible counsel for all of these positions.

I summarized how I felt about a half-dozen leading law firms, and specified what I thought were their strengths and weaknesses and how they met the criteria I'd outlined above. Under their strengths, I included the firms' ability to advise the board on its fiduciary duties in this situation, and to ensure that the steps the board and the individual directors might take were protected under the business-judgment rule. Potential weaknesses included whether or not individual law firms had previous or ongoing associations with HealthSouth.

I made my recommendation, but said I believed the final decision belonged to the board. Then I addressed another legal specialty that we'd be needing, a law firm with experience in criminal affairs to help us respond to the government's various investigations.

I think we really need to select new counsel. Again, my criteria are simply to find the best firm and people available, though an issue to consider is whether the key issues are civil liability (in which case we want a firm skilled in working with the SEC) or criminal (in which case we may want a different skill set).

Then I turned back to what I saw was another legal problem, though one of a different stripe:

Conclusions About the Role of Counsel at Board Meetings
Once we have selected counsel to fill this role, I think it is important that we all agree going forward about the role for lawyers at board meetings. I recognize that board members or groups of board members will retain counsel to advise them personally about the issues being faced; the number of lawyers and propriety of multiple counsel is a matter for another day. But I do not believe we can function effectively if every

board member has his or her own personal lawyer at every meeting. And I do not believe it is proper for the board to consider the views of each member's personal lawyer.

Therefore, I believe that the only counsel who routinely should attend our board meetings is our corporate, insolvency and fiduciary counsel. I believe we frequently will call on our regulatory and criminal counsel as well as our investigative counsel to attend all or part of board meetings.

The board had all these e-mails to consider overnight, once the meeting of the 20th was over. The directors were highly focused.

At that night's meeting (March 21st), I'm glad to say, the board did insist that the choice of a crisis-management team be put back on track, and one was selected soon after that. We also elected a lead law firm.

March 22 turned out to be my last day on the HealthSouth board. Strange though it seems, considering how important it was, I can't recall who gave me the information that led me to resign. In any event, I heard that Chubb, the insurance company that provided our D&O insurance, had returned HealthSouth's check and was canceling coverage. A phone call to the company confirmed that I was without coverage.

This was unacceptable, and various lawyers I called confirmed that I was putting all my personal assets at risk if I continued on the board. I had only one course of action, and called George Strong in his role as chair of the audit committee to say I was resigning, effective immediately. I called each of the directors that day to give my decision in person, and my reason for leaving. All the other directors felt they had to stay, the lack of D&O coverage notwithstanding. And all of them urged me to change my mind. When they saw that my decision was final, they thanked me for all I'd done.

I knew my departure would raise questions, or possibly be interpreted as a negative judgment on the company. But the risk and personal liability of continuing without insurance coverage was overwhelming. In fact, I've already been served with multiple lawsuits resulting from my brief time on the HealthSouth board.

I do take satisfaction from having made a contribution in that critical time by chairing the meetings and leading the agenda, collecting the information, and researching the alternatives for the decision-making process. Identifying the key steps and resources needed to stabilize the company, driving the decision to retain forensic accounting experts so we could get an accurate picture of HealthSouth's finances, and locating good crisis-management firms to facilitate and manage the key liquidity issues were valuable.

Some seven months later, things seem to be more stable. The investigations are continuing. Presumably the board still meets all the time and continues to work hard. Scrushy and Owens have been formally terminated. I see that Lee Hillman, former chairman and CEO of Bally Total Fitness, has joined the board and Richard Koppes a director of outstanding judgment and analytical skills, has joined. I wish them, and all the other board members, the very best.

Adapted from *Corporate Board Member* November/December 2003.

Nothing destroys shareholder value like a botched crisis response. Having a crisis management plan in place is as important as SOX 404 compliance. Tylenol's CEO led a stellar response and ended up making the brand even more trusted. You should insist on an annual run-through of the company's crisis management plan as part of "good corporate hygiene" to protect the shareholders.

Crisis Management and Your Board—Five Lessons from BP

When a major company combines extensive disaster management expertise with a world-class board of directors, what happens when a crisis strikes? Try asking BP. Although the company's Gulf Coast oil spill debacle now makes BP seem like the butt of crisis management jokes, just a year ago any corporate observer would anticipate the best from this massive multinational's board and management. Certainly the BP directors, with their global vitae and savvy, would insist that a company facing huge potential environmental exposures should have immediate plans to both prevent and manage a disaster. The board's fundamental risk management duties alone should see to that.

But no such sound crisis response plan was found at BP. Even in a sector where the company was most vulnerable to a disaster, a major oil spill, essential crisis planning was lax. In congressional hearings on the BP Gulf Coast disaster, U.S. Representative Ed Markey noted that BP's emergency oil spill plan was a near-duplicate of ineffective, boilerplate plans from several other petro companies—right down to a telephone number for an expert who'd died years earlier

Yet no board of directors should feel smug about how well their company has prepared for a crisis. As a member of many boards, from startups to major public companies, I've seen wide variation in how well management plans cope with a crisis. Worse, there are too many boards that never even *ask* about crisis plans. They have never properly considered and weighed the risks the company faces, much less how to respond.

This won't do anymore. Increasingly, the media, shareholders, regulators, and the wider public expect that a crisis should bring out the best in a corporation. The company's leaders should take center stage to prove themselves competent, in charge, concerned, and working effectively towards resolution. Further, "company leaders" today will include your board of directors. While BP CEO Tony Hayward was blasted for his public fumbles in dealing with the oil spill, the BP board (especially chairman Carl-Henric Svanberg) drew massive negative attention for their cluelessness. Solid crisis management planning can literally save your companies at such moments.

Crisis plans have several major elements, but the main two are internal and external. The internal crisis plans (what to do if the CEO dies, if your plant or product causes serious harm, if the company faces a major legal action, etc.) focus on technical, operational elements. Reviewing these is obviously a board duty. But then there is the external crisis management plan, dealing with investors, the media, and regulators, as well as company employees, suppliers, and the overall public. Here the board not only has an oversight duty, but, in today's corporate climate, a tactical, even personal, responsibility. While BP directors were probably wise not to head to Louisiana and offer to roll up their sleeves, they *did* have an important public role in the external crisis management. Their failure should serve as your example.

No doubt even a good crisis plan will not cover every contingency. The analogy of the "black swan," an event that is both dramatic and rare, has been much used since the financial crisis of 2008. Some business catastrophes, such as that facing BP, the Three-Mile Island nuclear leak, and the Union Carbide Bhopal chemical disaster, all combined one-in-a-million worst cases to occur. But "best practice" crisis management planning nurtures the resources, thinking and corporate muscles needed to respond to any crisis. As Dwight Eisenhower observed, "I have always found that plans are useless—but planning is indispensable."

I serve as a director with SunPower Corporation, a world leader in solar energy technology. The governance practices at SunPower have impressed me since I joined their board, and one aspect is their crisis management planning. Some crisis plans consist of a handful of clichés and a page of phone numbers (half of them no longer working). Not SunPower's plan. It's a 119-page document prepared by SunPower staff with assistance from Ogilvy PR, and breaks down who needs to do what for any company crisis. While this plan may sound lengthy, it's more of a guidebook, allowing anyone in company management or the board to look at the index and immediately "know their role."

Five Lessons

The SunPower Crisis plan, and the process used in shaping it, offers good ideas for all company leaders who realize that it's time to step up and create a workable crisis management plan. Here are five lessons that we learned in the process.

1. First is the most obvious, but essential—will your board and management make crafting a crisis response plan a priority? Will the funding and time be allotted, and management graded on effective completion?

This leads to various "first questions" your crisis plan must answer. What are the most likely crisis scenarios your company will face based on its industry, size, location, structure, vulnerabilities, etc.? The SunPower plan lists three tiers of crisis; emergency (dangerous, life-threatening situations), serious (threats to the company's operations or credibility), and newsworthy (some event, typically financial, that casts the company in a bad light). Thirteen examples, from a major plant catastrophe, to legal problems, to natural disasters, are offered.

Don't underestimate the practical efforts required to design a sound plan. Ingrid Ekstrom, corporate communications director for SunPower, led development of our crisis plan, and notes, "expect many rounds of internal review and approvals. Our plan was reviewed by representatives from several key areas of the company such as manufacturing and legal, as well as senior executives, requiring hours of coordination for the comments and reviews."

2. Does your plan designate outreach roles and messages for specific audiences (major investors, employees, the media, your relevant regulators, stock exchanges, local communities)? Who is to be the company's primary spokesman? Who is to be informed of what, when? What are the primary messages you'll need to deliver (continuity... public safety... maintaining shareholder value...)?

At SunPower, the crisis plan designates a three-person "Core Planning Team," with a further 32 top execs, department heads and board members as implementation and contact resources. Teams, checklists and sample "fill in the specifics" messages are included. One outstanding element of the plan is the extensive list of contacts included as appendices. This includes all the key crisis team members, as well as the company contact resources. It says a lot about how serious SunPower takes its crisis planning that even CEO Tom Werner lists his home and personal cell telephone numbers.

3. Does your plan consider various "scenario" options? Sure, it's standard procedure to designate your CEO as the primary spokesman. But what if the "crisis" facing your company is the sudden death of the CEO... or even the CEO's arrest or indictment? Too many corporations have been caught short when a "that will never happen to us" situation... happens. Make sure that your crisis communication plan builds in a "deep bench" of talent who will know their roles and messages if suddenly thrust into the spotlight. As important as designating who is the spokesperson, is a well-understood policy of who is *not* to talk to the press for the company. A strong policy of confidentiality is important.

4. Does the company have a pre-existing relationship with a proven crisis management publicity firm? At SunPower, we worked with the pro PR firm Ogilvy to craft our plan, and would be able to quickly tap their skills if demanded by an emergency.

Ability to view your company, its audiences, and communications challenges from the outside are further reasons why it can be wise to work with an outside counselor. Ingrid Ekstrom says, "Ogilvy helped us in framing the document and figuring out scenarios. We had tried a couple of different approaches on crisis management planning before, but using outside resources proved very helpful."

5. Finally, does your board of directors realize that its role in crisis management is subtly different from that of management? The tactical issues of working the problems at hand may overwhelm managers, or lead them to public statements that focus on legal, technical issues rather than those really concerning those outside the company. Remember how much technobabble BP was offering in the summer of 2010, when we all really just wanted to know when they were going to get the hole plugged?

More importantly, the board of directors has a fiduciary duty to protect the company's shareholder value and the public value of its brand.

Managers have these duties too, of course... but sometimes crisis response may tempt managers to focus first on protecting managers.

One last point for any crisis management plan—realize that your plan is never truly "completed." Remember Rep. Markey's comment above on the stale data in BP's emergency plan? It's easy to develop a document, and then forget about it while your company's people, contacts, strategy and exposures continue to evolve. "We include contact info for everyone, including top investors and the media," says Ekstrom. "Keeping your plan data updated is crucial."

Adapted from *Business-Ethics.com* November 8, 2010.

Global market sector shifts can trigger crisis as happened in 2000, when Lucent's revenue went from $33B to $8B in one year. Problems can cascade quickly—at Lucent we responded by holding almost weekly board meetings and taking the unusual step of self-reporting to the SEC, which was the right move at the time. But in hindsight we should have brought in more restructuring expertise and done the deep cuts at the beginning. My lesson learned is: make the biggest/hardest decisions as early as possible.

Companies in Crisis: A War Story from the Front Line

*Excerpted from the panel discussion at the 2002 Annual NACD Conference featuring panelist Betsy S. Atkins with **T. K. Kerstetter** Publisher, Corporate Board Member, as moderator. This panel features war stories from a true veteran.*

T.K. Kerstetter: Many companies today are struggling with financial problems and even scandals. Tyco, Global Crossing, Kmart—those are three companies that are so happy that Enron came along. Plenty of companies have examples of earnings restatements, frauds even bankruptcies that all put a board in crisis. Even companies missing the infamous "whisper number" by a penny or two have seen their stock plummeting. All of these can suddenly trigger a class action suit. You go onto the Web site of Milberg Weiss right now, there are 300 class action suits that investors can join through a box that asks, "Do you want to be part of one of these? Just click on the one you'd like to be a part of the class." All these situations can put a board in crisis. One of the things I ask Betsy not to miss out on is the emotion of this topic. I want her to start by just talking about an experience that they've had with a board in crisis, what the emotions were and what issues were raised while going through the crises—and then have her elaborate on what she has learned after having been through the process.

Betsy Atkins: The story that I'm going to share with you is the story of my two years as a director at Lucent, where we've gone through an enormous number of crises. So many crises, in fact, I actually had to write out my notes to be able to list them.

When I joined Lucent, it was not related to the company that I founded, Ascend, which had been previously acquired by Lucent. There was, in fact, a two-year hiatus. So, I came to Lucent knowing the company as a

37

very proud leading telecommunications vendor in America with one of the most famous research labs, Bell Laboratories. Upon my arrival, it was one surprise after another.

First of all, the telecommunications industry as a whole had an enormous turndown of 22 percent, which any of you who have been in a business know—a 22 percent implosion in your market is huge, especially when you're geared up for growth, which was the trajectory that everyone in our industry was on. Shortly following that, because of the way the telecommunications industry had been growing, a lot of the financing for the start-up telecommunications companies was through vendor financing. And once we got into that, we found out we had to restate earnings, which was followed by an investigation from the Securities and Exchange Commission.

Then we had a liquidity crunch and had to raise $6.5 billion under a lot of pressure and duress from 35 institutions. We also had to review our CEO and found that his skill set wasn't a match for the situation we were in. So we had to go through a CEO termination and get an acting CEO in place. We then, in survival mode and looking around the industry, felt that a cross-border international merger with Alcatel might be beneficial for both parties. So we entered into those negotiations but ended up terminating them. We also auctioned off two of our large divisions, each in excess of a billion dollars.

We then did an IPO spin-off of two major subsidiaries, Avaya, which is the handset PBX business, and Agere, the integrated circuit business. Both were approximately $5 billion. We had to integrate all of our acquisitions that we had made, where we had spent about $10 billion of shareholders' assets, and we wanted to be sure we'd get the value out of that. We also went through a major corporate restructuring, and we went from 123,000 employees down to 56,000. And the emotion involved in taking your workforce down and having to evaluate key corporate assets, like Bell Laboratories, which is a jewel in America, and ask ourselves how much basic research could we support versus how much product development was in the mix? All of this was followed by a shareholder lawsuit. So those were the first set of crises. In preparation for this panel, I asked myself what can I share with you that I've learned from this? And it's always embarrassing to show your scar tissue, but at least I now have experience. It's like getting a Ph.D. in board governance from this incredibly compressed timeframe of crises you could never have anticipated. The first thing we did was to *increase the frequency of our meetings* to a very high number. So in dealing with these crises, we ended up holding 58 board meetings last year—a record for one year! This necessitated rotating most of my other commitments, and I'm happy to say the restructuring is behind us, and it appears that we have stabilized. I think that that was the right way to approach crisis management—to proactively get out in front of it and really engage.

The next matter was the restatement of earnings. One of the actions taken that was extremely valuable for us was the very *active engagement of the audit committee* to look into all areas of revenue recognition, determine what was changing with vendor financing, and assess the strength of our internal financial controls and processes. So the aggressive stance of the audit committee was a very positive remedy.

Regarding the SEC investigation, *we took the initiative to communicate.* Once we delved into things, the audit committee uncovered some areas of concern. Then, we went to the SEC and got out in front of it, which I think is a very unusual thing. I don't know many boards and companies that actually go to the SEC before the SEC comes to them. I think that that was a very positive thing to do.

We *consciously evaluated and changed our tone at the top* in all of our financial areas. And during this process, we very consciously used outside counsel and were cognizant of process so that we would document and have an audit trail and made sure that we did everything possible that we could be doing. We documented our process because we knew there would be the inevitable and ugly shareholder lawsuit. For both our own comfort that we wanted to be sure there wasn't any steps that we missed—as well as for our future protection and defense— we created a very strong process.

As for the changing of the CEO, it's my own belief that by the time the boardroom starts to get a whiff that there's a problem with top leadership, the rest of the company is fainting from the smell and wishing the board would have gotten the message earlier. My opinion is—when you start to think there is something amiss, go and *investigate it actively.*

Regarding the restructuring, the same concept applies. As boards, we're not line managers. We understand that our role is governance, not in operations. But there can be a fine line. And in a restructuring, I think that the dynamics, the involvement, the level of engagement starts to shift when a company is in crisis. So if you have to go through a major restructuring, in hindsight, it would have been a lesson learned to have really taken the big cuts and made the related hard decisions as *early as possible* in the process—first for our own benefit, especially for the employees who suffer by the razor cuts and the anxiety of, "When will the next shoe fall and the next layoff come?" And for the benefit of the shareholders, who benefit when the restructuring is done earlier.

So, in closing, on my Lucent experience of dealing with crisis, I thought that the board was wise to be proactive and get very active in the number of meetings and get out in front of the issues as much as possible. And I thought that understanding that in a crisis, the normal distance of the board as governance versus line management becomes a little more blurred. Directors should be cognizant of that and be more engaged in a crisis environment.

Adapted from *Directors Monthly* July 2002 Annual Conference Edition.

Be sure your company is embracing key technology shifts to avoid a "Borders disaster," where leaders at Borders dismissed electronic books as a fad. You wouldn't approve an annual plan today if your company were not web enabled for Internet access by your prospects and customers. "Mobile" has the same mega impact as the web. Mobility must be actively adopted with easy to use, elegant applications for your customers and workforce if your company is to remain relevant. Request an update on your company's mobile and social strategy.

Avoid Serving on a Dinosaur Board

The term "macromyopia," also known as Amara's law, postulates that there is a tendency to overestimate the short-term impact of a new product or technology and underestimate its long-term implications on the marketplace, and how competitors will react. This concept perfectly describes the situation that many businesses face with the rapid—even exponential—onslaught of mobile technology expansion and adoption.

Despite economic woes, consumers are demonstrating an insatiable appetite for smartphones and next-generation tablets. According to IDC estimates, over 300 million smartphone devices were shipped in 2010, with projected growth of 55 percent for 2011. Tablet sales posted 80 percent year-over-year growth in the second quarter of 2011, according to Infonetics. The United Nations recently found that a staggering 85 percent of the world's population is now covered by a commercial wireless signal, which provides greater reach than the electrical grid.

With these infrastructure shifts, mobile devices are rapidly replacing traditional laptops and desktops at both home and work as the primary mechanism for accessing web-based content and applications. Research by mobile app developer AnyPresence indicates that mobile web users will surpass desktop users within years. Smartphone shipments in the U.S. and Europe have already surpassed regular mobile phones. Yet, surprisingly, most businesses still lack mobile support for both employee and customer-facing systems. Those who continue to underestimate this technological shift will quickly find themselves struggling for relevancy.

The most recent, well-publicized victim of this trend is Borders, whose failure to recognize the industry changing ramifications of mobile eBook readers resulted in them losing market share both to online entrants such as Amazon, and also to traditional competitors such as Barnes and Noble, who recently claimed a bold 25 per- cent of the eBook market. Even mobile technology stalwarts, Research In Motion and Nokia, missed the writing on the wall with respect to mobile ecosystem trends such as vibrant app stores and developer communities. Is your company vulnerable to the equivalent mobile disruption within your sector?

As a corporate director, it falls upon you to challenge the status quo of your firm's outlook with respect to leveraging and adapting to mobile trends for top-line growth and bottom-line efficiencies. One of the simplest litmus tests is to determine whether management has fully embraced the mobilization of enterprise applications, for both employee-facing (productivity- driven) and customer-facing (revenue and satisfaction-driven) business processes.

Mobility as a Service Channel

With the growing prevalence of web-connected mobile devices, consumers are increasingly be- ginning to transact with corporations through mobile channels before other methods of interaction. Customers and prospects using mobile-enabled web sites, and text messaging are gradually replacing traditional web and phone-based communication. IDC forecasts that mobile Internet users will grow at an annual compound rate of 16.6 percent through 2015 to surpass PC-based Internet users.

Every facet of business, especially those with customer touch points such as marketing and service, will have to adapt and become mobile-ready. The reality is that most businesses are not prepared for this post-PC world: more than 65 percent of companies have not yet implemented a mobile marketing strategy, according to Hubspot and Google reports that almost 80 percent of large advertisers do not have a mobile-optimized web site. This means that as more customers conduct a search on their mobile device to find your business, the vast majority are not getting a mobile optimized experience, which can severely damage a brand. Just as companies who were slow to respond to web adoption in the 90s played catch-up, those who miss this rapid shift to mobility will be left further behind.

In addition to being able to reach prospects through a critical new channel, mobility provides a compelling opportunity for businesses across many industries to both improve customer satisfaction and lower the cost of customer service. The latter benefit is particularly important for bottom line savings during uncertain economic times.

Take, for example, energy providers in the utilities sector. Most energy providers have a captive audience, but in order to raise rates while avoiding the ire of regulators and politicians, they must ensure high levels of customer satisfaction. The ability to serve energy customers via mobile web and text-messaging channels presents a tremendous opportunity for utilities to provide more proactive information about outages, power restoration times, bill payment options and other self-service capabilities. Not only does this channel result in higher levels of customer satisfaction, it also has the potential to generate tremendous savings due to inbound call-center volume reduction.

This dual benefit of cost reduction and customer satisfaction awaits companies that are prepared to invest and innovate around mobile web-enabling their customer-facing processes. Those who fall behind will quickly find themselves facing the prospect of having fewer customers to service at all.

Mobility for Workforce Productivity
An interesting workforce demographic shift is underway that already significantly impacts the foundation of employee facing information technology. As baby boomers begin to retire in greater numbers, the millennial generation—those born in the 1980s and 90s—will comprise at least 50 percent of the workforce by 2014. This increasingly younger workforce has grown up with Internet-connected mobile devices, social networks and personal productivity tools. They expect the same level of technology as they enter the workplace to interact with each other and customers to remain productive.

Sure, your current HR system or traditional intranet site may seem like a "good-enough" solution today. How do you think this new workforce, who bring their personal mobile devices to work with hyper-connected expectations, will react to an antiquated system that cannot even support the most simple tasks as looking up a colleague's profile or submitting a vacation request on their mobile device?

Accenture recently published a research study on how younger employees use information technology in the workplace. Within the U.S., more than one in three consider state-of-the-art technology to be "essential when choosing an employer." This finding should be considered a wake-up call to most corporations. If you expect to be able to recruit and retain talent, you must have a modern, "consumerized" IT infrastructure.

The same study also finds that 77 percent of young employees feel that "technology helps improve the quality of my work," 76 percent feel "technology helps me be more successful in my career," and 73 percent find that "technology makes it easier to communicate with my peers and supervisors." The implication is clear: younger employees in particular require modern technology not simply because they feel it is "cool," but more practically because it supports the way they work. This reality is already well known to companies in the high technology and services-based industries, whose workforce is composed primarily of multi-generational knowledge workers, often in dispersed offices around the globe. Consider fast-growing startups such as LivingSocial, adding employees at a breakneck pace of 500 percent within a year. This type of organization will need to leverage advances in technology both to recruit and retain talent in a highly competitive sector.

Mobilize or Perish
As the economy improves and the war for talent and customers continues to expand across all sectors, corporations will rapidly lose their competitive edge if they have not modernized both their customer and employee-facing technology infrastructure to support mobile channels. As company directors and board members who seek to follow principles of sound governance, we must continuously challenge management to ensure the long-term health and competitiveness of our corporations. Part of this responsibility is to ask whether the customer service and human resource departments, in particular, are aware of mobility trends affecting their respective areas and embracing mobile technology ensures competitiveness. If your corporation is not providing cutting-edge mobile technology to serve your customers and employees, there are plenty of more nimble competitors who will.

Adapted from NACD: *The Director's Chair* March/April 2012.

Opinion: Companies Must Adapt to the Blurring of Silos

The digital industrial revolution has blurred business lines and altered what "buying" and "employment" mean. Boards that are rooted in the past will get left behind. Instead, they need to ensure their management team is positioned to be flexible.

Everything is blurring

Silos are being destroyed, such as with a blurring of lines between marketing/communications and engineering. For example, a Chief Marketing Officer needs to be able and willing to bring marketing and engineering teams together, which can result in product teams becoming more nimble and consumer-insight-driven. Digital marketing using data mining and analytics will require investment in experiment-driven marketing and research, either through building internal capabilities or partnering with specialists. This kind of work will demand executive-level acceptance of small failures as part of uncovering scalable opportunities. Building a corporate culture of experimenting will yield fast wins or fast fails through quick proof of concepts, which can help companies innovate and then move forward.

Not only are lines blurring between business units, but the lines between how companies sell and how customers transact are also changing. On the United Airlines app, for example, you can book a plane and book an Uber. And social media platforms are already tying e-commerce features into their networks. From Instagram 's "Shop Now" to Pinterest's "Buyable Pins," today's hot platforms are blurring the lines between Web, social, app and e-commerce. This is only going to speed up, and boards need to review whether their management teams are on top of this phenomenon.

The Sharing Economy and the Gig Economy

Globally, the sharing economy was around $15 billion in 2014, and it is projected to reach $335 billion by 2025. The success of companies such as Uber, Airbnb , Thumbtack and TaskRabbit aren't a fad; it's new way of doing business. These companies created affordable solutions for cash-strapped consumers to connect with individuals looking to provide services, which has the dual effect of changing how people purchase things and creating unique income streams for those offering their services. And the sharing economy's story doesn't end with taxis and vacation rentals. As consumers share and recycle their belongings, overall product demand might decrease. If that happens, companies will compete with millions of consumers willing to rent the same products they sell for a fraction of the cost.

Related to the sharing economy, the gig economy has emerged, where workers pick up shifts like a musician booking a gig. Now and increasingly in the future, companies won't hire head count directly. Instead, they'll outsource it, either through gigs or through companies like Global Logic that do outsourced software product development. Millennials are now the largest segment of our workforce, and many are freelancers, who overall make up 34% of the workforce. Employment will become increasingly uncoupled as more opportunity for flexible part-time work becomes available. Millennials also want to work for and purchase from companies with more authenticity and transparency. Without a clear purpose and high ethical standards, companies will find themselves floundering. To meet this need, companies need to create a culture of external orientation. Focus on your customers' needs and desires first, and then build a set of tactics and strategy around this.

Companies will also need faster innovation around the edges and quicker trials that answer certain questions: Did we solve the problem or not? How do we make it better? And how do we learn faster and iterate more often?

To meet these challenges, boards must take on a new strategic oversight role, encouraging management to actively listen and seek out these new macro innovation trends around digitization, customer-centric experiences, cross-silo collaboration, fast experimentation and the sharing and gig economy. Boards must also evaluate their CEO in light of this new reality.

A best practice for boards is to specifically request that management present the company's plans on how it will deal with these fast-moving innovations. Doing so demonstrates that the board is evolving beyond oversight to become a competitive asset for the company and its shareholders.

Adapted from *Agenda Magazine* May 31, 2016 Edition.

Learning from United's PR Disaster: Four Board Tips for "Re-accommodating" Crisis

If you serve on the corporate board of United Airlines, this week started badly and quickly grew far worse. The ugly incident of a passenger being dragged off an overbooked United flight not only showed a company that's lost its way on "customer service," but also one that badly botched its response in today's instant social media world.

You already know the details—a Sunday flight from Chicago to Louisville was overbooked, and United staff sought passengers willing to make room for a United flight crew needed in Louisville. One passenger, bumped at random, refused to leave, and airline security manhandled him, dragging him off the plane streaming blood.

United board members woke up to this news Monday, including a video taken by a passenger that quickly went viral. #United has been a top twitter trend since then (never a good sign), and massive negative news coverage led to a national spasm of outrage.

It endlessly puzzles me that major firms, even those with a life-or-death need for good consumer relations, so often botch major media crises. And these debacles are not just a few days of minor bad news any more. Twenty-four hours after the United beat-down story broke, the company's stock price had dropped three percent—$600 million in shareholder value lost.

What lessons can companies and their boards draw from this "fly the unfriendly skies" disaster?

Have a crisis plan in place.
I wrote that twice because too many boards and managements still ignore this obvious need. Any consumer-facing business (which today is pretty much every business) must have a prearranged crisis escalation protocol in place for dealing with consumer incidents. Sure, major legal, leadership or product crisis plans are things any company should already have ready to roll. But what about dealing with an isolated consumer incident, something that's easy to dismiss or ignore—until it explodes. Then, within hours, a social media and news storm can put the company's brand itself in peril.

47

Work out a plan that details who is monitoring the social media matrix for such issues, how leadership will be apprised of flare-ups, and what steps and messages will be sent, and how. Run fire drills on a regular basis to make sure a smart response becomes basic muscle memory for staff.

Seek outside help

Your company media relations and IR staff may object, but I advise prearranging support from a proven outside communications firm. As good as your internal media team may be, outside specialists have strong, real-time media relations contacts, and professional crisis management firms are constantly on the firing lines in spotting (and solving) sensitive public and political crises. They should be the ones alerting you to a blowup involving your public image.

Embrace the leadership test.

Board members look to the CEO when a public crisis strikes, and the CEO's poise and messages determine how long he or she stays employed. While the United incident should never have happened, CEO Oscar Munoz compounded the problem with a lawyered-up statement about the unfortunate need to "re-accommodate" passengers (giving Twitter a whole new hashtag to play with). Plus, in a private email to United staff (assume in today's world there is never such a thing as a private email), Munoz told staff that he had their back when dealing with "disruptive and belligerent" passengers.

Assess board disaster skills

Rosanna Landis Weaver, of the As You Sow social investing service (http://ceopay.asyousow.org/2017/04/united-airlines/), writes that the United Airlines board includes heavy corporate hitters with vitae in such fields as aircraft technology, finance, and corporate strategy. What's missing? How about directors with customer service expertise, and first-hand knowledge of dealing with consumers? If your board has no one who brings deep consumer perspective/expertise, expect customers to be treated as afterthoughts.

United Airlines is far from the only company to face a sudden, social-media consumer sinkhole. Uber, Wells Fargo, Volkswagen and too many other major firms have seen their brands suffer due to hubris, complacency and lack of skills. But such crises offer the rest of us vital lessons on the power of our customers, and the urgency of brand image in our social media age.

Adapted from *Directors & Boards Online* April 13, 2017.

CHAPTER 3: GOVERNANCE MATTERS

In a macroeconomic crisis like the 2008 upheaval, boards need to help management focus on the long-term competitive health of the company. Don't arbitrarily cut all budgets by a fixed percent; focus on operational efficiencies like editing low-margin, low-volume SKUs (Stock Keeping Units) and continue to reward performance to retain top talent in difficult times.

The duty of care is a director's biggest responsibility: to carefully protect the interests of the shareholders. Always document the logic behind decisions, use outside un-conflicted experts, document the deliberations of the decisions, and create a record to refresh/remind you in case of litigation. A great process will help you reach the best decision; don't be rushed.

Performing the Duty of Care: A Director's Perspective

In the wake of the most recent wave of corporate scandals, nearly all of the resulting lawsuits have alleged that the directors did not carefully protect the interest of the shareholders. They allege that directors violated their most important duty, the duty of managing the oversight of the company's business on behalf of the shareholders. This is called the duty of care. There are a number of specific steps that directors can undertake to help them prove that they are performing their duty of care.

Document Your Thinking for Any Decisions in the Board's Books
The board's books should contain a clear answer of the logic behind any major decision—the decisions that have significant economic or strategic consequences. The directors should look back and ask: What facts, what analysis, and what expert advice did we receive when we made that

decision? It is very important that the corporate secretary have a retention policy—that is consistently followed—to carefully prepare, review, and preserve the board books so that you will have good documentation in the event that your decisions are challenged. You must make sure that your decisions are made with comprehensive, thoughtful preparation with adequate background material. The decisions should be accompanied by a recommendation from management. The board's books should contain management's recommendation and the basic background and analytical information that management relied on when reaching their recommendation.

The Board's Books Should Be Drafted for Two Audiences
This one is key. The board's books should be drafted for potential plaintiffs, particularly where there is a decision that later could be challenged if the execution of the business strategy is not successful. To give you the most protection possible, it is desirable to ask management to summarize the pros and cons of different alternatives and then identify why management made a particular recommendation.

Ensure That the Experts That the Board Relies on Truly Are Qualified
Under state law, directors are able to rely on experts, but this reliance needs to be reasonable. To be confident that the directors can rely on a particular set of experts, it is important that they have the appropriate credentials, experience, and background for the subject matter at hand. These credentials ought to be included in the board's books. An important part of making sure that your experts truly meet the criteria of giving sound advice is to ascertain that they are not conflicted at all, including that there is no potential conflict of interest. If there is a potential conflict of interest and the board decides to rely on the expert anyway, the board must probe to ensure that the expert has the ability to rise above the potential conflict of interest. In the fairness opinion context, it is best to have the opinion delivered by an investment bank that is different from the one that receives the success fee for having the transaction completed. The board can do this by restricting the investment bankers when they sign their engagement letter. Overall, you should put together a checklist of questions that reassures the directors that they are getting independent expert advice. If you document a brief checklist like this in the board's books, then it demonstrates the care the directors are taking when they make their business judgments.

Take Your Time if Possible

It is very important to make sure that the directors take adequate time to really think about, discuss, ask questions, and really absorb critical information before making a business decision. This is a critical element of showing due care. When there is a large amount of information that has to be analyzed for an immediate decision, it is not uncommon for the decision in hindsight to be challenged. As a result, it is critical to hold multiple board meetings before making a major business decision. For these meetings, it is up to the directors to set the tone for requesting the appropriate information in advance so that they are not put into the position of making a shotgun decision. If management claims that there is a short deadline for decision-making, directors should ask why there is such urgency. Will delaying the decision materially change the tax implications or change a price in negotiation? Will a competitor enter the scene? Is there a change in law about to occur? If one of these major reasons is not present, then it is important to push back and take more time to enable the board to place more careful thought into the decision. If there is an imperative timetable, then it is important to document this urgency as well as to document that careful thought still went into the ultimate decision. Think about your decisions in hindsight, would a jury member analyzing massive amounts of data be able to make an informed decision? This is probably what a plaintiff's attorney would ask. Directors must be able to demonstrate a deliberate process in reaching their conclusions.

Hire Experts When Needed

Obviously, each director cannot be an expert in every matter that they must analyze for the company. More than ever, boards are seeking opinions from accountants, industry experts, and compensation experts when appropriate to help them make informed decisions. It is important that directors get an expert opinion when they need one, even if these opinions are expensive. However, directors can obtain expert opinions in cost-effective ways. For example, the cost of a fairness opinion varies considerably based on the balance sheet strength of the firm giving the opinion. A regional investment banking firm might charge half for a fairness opinion compared to a Wall Street firm. By using a regional firm, directors still have a professional opinion that provides a protective shield. Sometimes you can find people with investment banking expertise that charge on an hourly basis and can provide the board with the type of analysis that can serve as additional information that the board considers.

By having this information in the boards' possession and memorializing this reliance, an expert witness would be able to identify this analytical information that was available to the board in any litigation and show that the board was careful when making its decision.

In the five points covered above there is a clear pattern for the directors to establish so that they are insulated from lawsuits. This pattern shows that important decisions were made carefully and thoughtfully, so that the duty of care, to conscientiously protect the corporation, demonstrates the directors' thought process behind their business decisions and conclusions.

Most importantly the directors minimize the chance of reaching a bad decision when they have a process of collecting objective outside information and utilizing experts:

First, document the analysis that went into the decision and the recommendations made to the board. Then, keep records that show the board reviewed and understood the expertise and credentials of experts prior to their being hired. This shows that the board made sure the experts had both capabilities and independence in their recommendations. Finally, be sure to take the time to pull together information and analyze this before reaching a conclusion so that you can show both in reality as well as appearance that you discharged your duty of care.

The directors are responsible for putting their most thoughtful analysis into their business judgment and their business decisions. It is important that the board feels that they were prudent and careful and decided things "in good faith and on reasonable grounds." It is also important in principle that the directors can show that they deliberated carefully and demonstrate that they were diligent in arriving at their decisions. It is possible that a court would try to second-guess a director's decision, so being able to show the extent of the information on which the decision was based is very important.

The key is the process of careful thoughtfulness that the board went through in evaluating the facts before reaching their decisions. This will make sure that even if the decision has turned out to be faulty, the directors will be protected by being able to demonstrate that they discharged a duty of care in arriving at their at their business decision.

Boards must show that they acted in what they believe to be the best interest of the company based on all of the facts, as they existed at the time when the decision was made. Directors need to make "reasonable" decisions, not perfect decisions. By showing the support and background for how they made their "reasonable decision," directors can feel confident that they will ultimately be protected as having discharged their duty of care in reaching their business decision.

Adapted from *Corporate Governance Advisor* May/June 2004.

Economic Turmoil Changes Director Focus

We are in an economic upheaval and the oversight that the board provides during this time will influence the company for years ahead. We as board members need to be active in helping management focus on the opportunity that this market crisis brings beyond our normal oversight of budgetary review, cost containment, business strategy, etc.

Usually in an upheaval people get a "bunker" mentality and become defensive. Our role is to motivate the company to look across a wide range of topics from product development, market share growth, talent top grading, cost management, and review of the full range of risks.

We need to focus on the risks that are the most likely ones to impact our businesses, and the areas where we can drive the biggest long-term returns. We must look forward for efficiencies, and focus on the cost of goods sold (COGS).

Drive Cost Efficiency

Traditionally, management and boards look at cutting costs in market slowdowns. Rather than taking costs out of general and administrative (G&A) funds, cost trimming is most effective if we focus on identifying cost reductions that may be within the COGS. Companies that trim and improve their operational efficiency yield longer lasting financial results, positioning the company to be stronger. Companies should:

- Review and edit low margin stock keeping units (SKUs)
- Be creative in pricing models to generate additional revenue
- Develop joint business/marketing agreements for cost effective incremental revenue
- Work with vendors to share future inventory needs, thereby allowing them to plan and capture efficiencies that can benefit you both
- Create longer term contracts in inventory.

A key way for companies to save on COGS is to get rid of the unprofitable products. It's important to look at the "total costs of capital" when calculating the profitability of each SKU. Oftentimes, cost accounting systems don't capture capital costs, and less profitable SKU's end up staying in the product line when they should not. Now that capital is not readily accessible and very expensive, companies should definitely look at the "cost of capital" when they review their SKUs.

Preserve Investment Areas

Companies must continue to invest in the growth areas for their future. It is a mistake to take a numerical approach and cut all capital expenses as a percentage across all areas, or to decide to defer capital projects. A better approach is to decide what are the differentiated unique growth initiatives for the company, and exempt those projects from budget cuts. Companies need to look at a budget review with two things in mind: cost savings opportunities, and future growth initiatives.

Investors expect well-run companies to continue to perform (versus their competition), even in a downturn. Companies need to communicate to the investors that they are going to continue investing in differentiated strategic projects that are unique innovations for the company's future. The board needs to encourage management to be long term, not only short term. The board can encourage management to identify the "business owners" of the projects who will then determine the tradeoffs within their budget, to drive results for the best return. Companies that invest effectively in growth and future innovation need to encourage innovative thinking in all company functions, including marketing, manufacturing, procurement, and IT, and not just within the R&D group. Fostering a culture within the company to create differentiated and uniquely valuable products and services will keep employees motivated through a downturn for a positive future.

Conserve Cash

Cash is tight now for both companies and their customers. Companies need to be thoughtful and come up with new offerings that may allow customers the ability to purchase a product or service in smaller increments. The customer may be willing to pay slightly more up front, or per unit, in order to purchase a smaller quantity or size of the total order. Customers may also be willing to pay a premium for their product or service if the company has a long track record of being very reliable, or able to guarantee supply.

This same concept applies to how companies can conserve their cash in working with their suppliers. Pushing suppliers to continue supplying inventory in smaller quantities rather than consuming a company's cash too quickly will be key in this time of tight credit.

Check Contracts for Honey Pots

Boards should encourage management to have an open discussion in the leadership team, and reach a consensus on what key risks could impact the business. There may be a range of differing views within management on where the risks lie, as well as appetite levels to take on risk.

Opportunities come out of economic downturns. A company with a strong balance sheet might use its cash to lower their prices and capture market share, or offer financing for clients that competitors cannot offer. The risks from suppliers as well as business partners can be addressed by broadening the number of vendors or partners. Procurement and legal functions are areas that may provide management with some positive opportunities in this downturn by providing careful review of contracts to see if there are any terms or covenants that are now enforceable that the company may want to use to their advantage. For example, sometimes contracts that are no longer deemed beneficial can be voided due to credit ratings, debt covenants, or inability to raise capital. A careful review of the company's current, past, and future contracts may identify pockets of opportunity.

The board needs to encourage management to be vigilant on ethics and compliance in economic downturns. Incidents of internal theft, fraud, and insider trading typically rise in tough times. Management may wish to get out in front of this, and reinforce their policies.

Pay the Performers

This market downturn creates an outstanding opportunity for top-grade talent. There is more talent available out in the market and more importantly, often the best talent, which was not looking, is now recruitable. Boards should actively request management to carefully review their leadership team, and trade up their middle performers. This is a great time to find scarce skills if the company can offer a persuasive picture of their future.

Recognition and compensation for outstanding performers must continue in tough times. The instinct may be to cut compensation across the board, and this is a huge mistake. The shareholders' interests are always served when the high performers are rewarded. There is an enormous difference in the results that great performers contribute, versus average performers. Employees all know who the star performers are, and they will be motivated to see recognition and rewards for top contributors.

Compensation committees do need to be thoughtful and make sure that their pay plans are clear and transparent, and easily understood by the shareholders. The pay plans should be aligned long term with shareholder interests, i.e. total shareholder return, market share, and other metrics versus shorter-term earnings-per-share-only reward systems. The best compensation committees compare their executives against peer groups, and look at each piece of the pay package—base, bonus, and equity— and annually review their compensation philosophy. This year, special programs may be needed such as a CEO discretional equity pool to get through these tough times.

The management team that successfully works together identifying crisp plans to lead the company forward, and capturing new competitive opportunities, will have gained unique experience in working through a market downturn. The highest potential managers will shine, and the team will have sharpened its decision-making and business judgment capabilities.

Keeping the morale high and management focused on the important priorities of balancing costs against future growth opportunities is a key role for the board to deliver the right results for the shareholders.

Adapted from *Directors Monthly* February 2009.

Boards have a personality, either open or closed. The problem of a rogue or disruptive director needs to be proactively and diplomatically addressed by the lead director or chairman.

When a Board Colleague Goes Rogue

Boards have personalities. They are open, interactive, and engaged ... or formal, command and control environments. Obviously there are many shades of gray in between, but these predominant board personalities can be significantly impacted by a "rogue" director.

The problem of a director becoming a rogue who takes on too much power, authority and decision-making, or becomes loquacious, disruptive and argumentative, is significantly worsened and exacerbated in a command and control board environment.

Open, engaged board environments are fostered when the lead director makes sure that each member of the board can participate and is heard, and can actively contribute. When all members participate you create a bonding or "processing as a team," and this positive peer pressure keeps any single member from going rogue by taking too much power, making too many decisions, or becoming argumentative and disruptive.

When a colleague becomes rogue it really is the responsibility of the lead director or governance chair to invest the time to have a series of discussions to help that colleague to modify their negative behavior. There needs to be time invested to gradually bring this colleague back into a productive behavior mode. This can only be accomplished by investing the time to build enough of a trusted communication and rapport to help reshape the negative behavior.

Ultimately, if the rogue director can't be modified then it may be necessary to not ask that director to stand for reelection. It is important when delivering the message that a director is not going to be invited to re-stand to try to shape this in a way that preserves the rogue director's "face" and dignity. Be as gracious as possible in representing the company's deep appreciation for their past service.

When delivering the message that a director will not be invited to re-stand it is essential that this be presented as an absolute conclusion, so there is no misunderstanding, and to minimize awkwardness. This past director will remain connected out in the industry, so it is important to do "preventive damage control" for the company's reputation, and that this transition be as smooth as possible.

Adapted from *Directors & Boards* Second Quarter 2012.

CHAPTER 4: BUILDING A BETTER BOARD

Boards should be renewed with different/new skills over time just as management teams are: market conditions change and company business models adapt to them. Board composition may need updating for many reasons; for example, companies going through large setbacks in revenue may need restructuring expertise.

Board Renewal as a Strategic Differentiator Driving Success

Public company directors know that our most important responsibility to the shareholders is succession planning and continuity of leadership to build and lead the enterprise. We are in a time of great market upheaval and pressure. This will require many corporations to adjust and change their business model. They will need to cut costs and think more broadly about how to compete to build and preserve shareholder value.

All directors clearly understand the importance of having a robust pool of general managers to develop and cultivate for leadership succession. When the CEO hires a senior executive to build the leadership team we are actively involved. We understand that corporations outgrow the capabilities of their executives. Hiring and promoting talent to adjust to a new business model enables the company to grow and adapt to changing business environments.

Although a board faces the same outside pressures, board succession is almost never discussed. It is one of the taboos in the boardroom, yet the perspective around the boardroom table must change with time. Just as a company may outgrow its CEO, the company also may outgrow the capabilities of its board members.

61

Companies that engage in board renewal find that it brings a set of experiences, perspectives and an important network of introductions and contacts. A positive example can be seen at SunPower Corp. The board was small when SunPower, a solar panel systems company, went public in 2005 with three outside board members.

SunPower's business evolved; we acquired and integrated companies and began the process of expanding our thinking on offshoring our manufacturing, tightening our supply chain, and globalizing our go-to-market. We recruited Dr. Uwe-Ernst Bufe, former CEO of Degussa, a global chemical company, to help mentor our CEO and bring contacts and expertise in the polysilicon supply chain, as well as deep operational knowledge.

SunPower then adapted its business model, expanding to sell its solar panels from residential, to business rooftops and to joint venturing with utilities. We needed depth, experience, and knowledge in the utilities sector, and added Tom McDaniel, former EVP and CFO of Edison International. This is an example of building a board and forward investing in it to bring knowledge, direct experience, contacts, and what I characterize as "scar tissue," to the boardroom. The board is truly in a partnership, to mentor and contribute actively with our CEO and his leadership team.

A contrary example can be seen at Lucent, where I was a board member in 2000. Lucent went through an enormous market challenge when the telecom industry imploded and revenues went from $33 billion to $8 billion in one year. Clearly, bringing in a board member who had gone through market dislocations and financial restructuring would have enhanced the company's ability to remain viable, strengthened the CEO's knowledge, and allowed the company to make the necessary aggressive decisions in order to endure and evolve. Rather than do that, the company brought on a NASA scientist who had never been in the for-profit product world, which was clearly not the perspective needed.
I believe companies and shareholders are well served when boards actively engage in board renewal. Just as CEOs look at the management team and see who would scale and who would not, and what is needed to maximize the enterprise performance in a marketplace, the same analysis should be applied to board members.

Annual board assessments usually focus on the information that management supplies the board and whether it is received in a timely manner. What boards may better ask themselves is whether the board can be strengthened—what new perspectives and experience would help our enterprise going forward? If this question is asked, we may see more board renewal in the future.

Adapted from *Chief Executive* June 2009.

What Makes a Great Board?

Q: How do newly public companies go about constructing a board?

A: Think about building a new board the way one would for a leadership team. It's important to recruit people who have professional experience going through similar stages of growth that the company will experience in the next three to five years. For example, if the company is going public and it's generating about $100 million in revenue, recruit board members who have experience being an active and engaged board member for a company that went from $100 million in revenue to $500 million or $1 billion in revenue. Because if you only brought on board members who had been on very large companies, that's a problem. The journey of growing from $1B to $15B is a very different journey than $100M to $500M. The corporate structure is different for a large global multinational with a big complex matrix organization.

Q: How does a company determine the right mix of skill sets and talent for the board?

A: The company's first step is to figure out what they need, ask yourself to think about the functional capabilities and expertise that will accelerate its business and then try to map that to the attributes of board members who bring different and complimentary perspectives to the discussion. A company will need board members or two or three with experience that is well matched to the organization's current and upcoming stages of growth. Companies may want to have a sitting or former CEO among the mix. Companies should also look for one or two people with deep domain expertise that understand their business. If the company is in the ad tech, cybersecurity, or industrial business, for example, they will want at least one or two members who either come from that specific industry or have been in related, adjacent industries with customers that are similar to the ones they are targeting. Companies may also find it valuable to have people whose experience in the "partner eco system" of the company's distribution model. For example, if the company is a retailer, it needs board members with retail experience, even if it's not in that same exact retail category. There will be parallels, for example, between women's apparel and men's apparel, for example. Similarly, a company might find it valuable to add a board member who has been in the ecommerce business, if the company has identified this as an important area of growth for its distribution channel. Alternatively, it might want somebody in the social media and content creation business because it wants to engage and influence buyers.

Q: Is the process different for recruiting new talent for an established board?

A: Yes, the challenges are very different for a large cap multinational corporation. These companies may have moved through the growth company stage and are possibly into the value company stage. Value companies, such as Proctor & Gamble and Kimberly Clark, grow at about 5% per year compared to a new Nasdaq IPO that has growth objectives of 25% to 35% per year.

The type of organizational structure, the amount of change that a corporation goes through, is very different in a high growth company than in a large cap value company. The challenges the business is facing are very different. It's important to look for different perspectives as a company populates its board and renews its board as it goes through different stages of growth.

Q: For established companies, what is the best approach to board refreshment?

A: The Board's governance committee, which typically includes governance and nominations, should look at the Board's individual and collective skill set annually with an eye toward creating a matrix of the skills that the company thinks it will need in the next three to five years.
For example, most companies don't have enough experience in digitization, digital transformation, or technology. Pretty much every business today is going through a digital transformation of some kind and needs to understand how to monetize their "Big Data" through analytics, implement distributed global computing and secure mobile access, whether it is doing business by ecommerce or using ecommerce as a way to take cost out of the supply chain.

Sometimes an assessment is forced on a board if the company is underperforming, and the shareholders will provide feedback on what they think the board is missing. If a company is really underperforming, activists will get involved and certainly they will make it known what they think the company board skill set is missing. The practical advice on how to actually execute board refreshment is another conversation. It's definitely awkward and contentious. Your Board Chairman needs to have the fortitude to look at a fellow member and say to them, "You were really a fantastic board member for ten years, but for the next five we need somebody different." Board renewal is an art. It is going to be uncomfortable, but it is important to go about it in a professional and nonpersonal manner without bruising egos.

Q: What do you think about the role of proxy advisory firms in reviewing boards? Do they serve a constructive purpose?

A: Proxy advisory firms have tried to make things so formulaic that their approach doesn't fit all situations. I do think that there's some value, because the institutional shareholders, the big ones like Fidelity and State Street, listen and act on their recommendations voting their shares based on the opinions expressed by ISS. So they're very powerful. If ISS says "your board is stale, and you need to rotate in some new members," it may trigger board renewal. And by and large there's value in all organizations, at all levels, to occasionally renew themselves. This is true whether it's a management team or a board.

Q: How do you feel about the current pressure to disclose board evaluations and corporate governance guidelines in proxy statements?

A: The Board has a difficult task of looking at themselves and saying, "We don't really have great strength in this area or that area." It's a hard process for any group to evaluate itself objectively and come up with an action plan. More disclosure is inevitable so it may make sense for companies to proactively embrace some additional disclosure related to board assessment and refreshment. Large institutional shareholders are going to demand it, as they are no longer going to be passive index fund owners. They're going to require companies to disclose much more going forward, which will likely ensure board assessment and refreshment will happen more frequently.

Q: Statistics show that newly public companies typically have a smaller percentage of women on boards than larger enterprises. What advice do you have for newly public companies on identifying and recruiting qualified female candidates?

A: There are many companies that specialize in recruiting and promoting women board members, like Trewstar and Kingsley Gate. And there's a new sort of LinkedIn version of finding board members, called ExecRank, which offers access to a pool of tens of thousands of qualified women director candidates. So there's a variety of ways for companies to identify qualified women candidates.

Q: There is a perception in corporate America that there aren't enough qualified women candidates in the talent pool, impeding progress toward parity in the boardroom. Do you agree?

A: I believe there are plenty of talented and capable women director candidates. There's no lack of talent. As part of a company's board refreshment, they need to make gender diversity part of their focus. I'm actually optimistic that it's going to happen because institutional shareholders who have the most influence, like State Street, Vanguard, and Fidelity, are all stating that they want to see gender diversity. Just 15 years ago they were more passive, but that's not the case anymore. They now have very robust governance groups. Certainly, Anne Sheehan of CalSTRS is a marvelous example of explaining what her pension fund wants to see in the boardroom. I believe this is going to drive change in a positive and much quicker way than it has in the past.

Adapted from *Nasdaq Spotlight* July 11, 2016.

7 Critical Elements of a Board Refreshment Plan

1) View the corporate board as a strategic asset, not just a fiduciary

The first step to an effective board refreshment plan is understanding why refreshment is so important. Historically, the function of boards was to act as a financial fiduciary and steward for shareholders. However, for the past decade or so, the role of boards has been evolving as boards are being held for futureproofing against threats and ensuring the competitive relevance of the organization.

Just as a company's leadership team is forward-hired based on long-term strategy, the board is now equivalently an asset to be reviewed for critical expertise and experience, and refreshed as needed. Unfortunately, it's still not common for a board to have a holistic view of board composition as a strategic asset, and many corporate boards still view themselves as fiduciaries.

2) Take a proactive versus reactive approach.

It's never been more important to address the topic of refreshment internally- if the board doesn't proactively think about it, somebody outside the organization is going to raise it. Index funds that were traditionally passive are now beginning to push for diversity, governance refreshment and renewal, and are raising questions on term limits and age limits.

A board should have an annual governance committee calendar with explicit agenda items, just as it does for compensation committees and audit committees. A typical governance committee refreshment calendar might run as follows:

- ✓ Q1: Review board composition, long-term succession, planning and rotation schedules.
- ✓ Q2: Map board skill sets to the corporation's long-term strategic plan.
- ✓ Q3: Review the board skills matrix to identify gaps.
- ✓ Q4: Outline a plan for executing graceful rotations and engaging search firms to assist in filling gaps.

A standardized annual process for board refreshment establishes expectations on term limits from the beginning, ensures recruitment of new members is not a shotgun affair, and takes the personal element out of rotating members off the board. Board refreshment becomes a pure, professional process for identifying and filling needed skill sets.

3) Annually map board skill sets against the company's long-term strategic plan

In the absence of a detailed vision of board composition, it's human nature to place a premium on good working relationships. That's why so many boards report that they turn to their own networks to recruit new members. Therefore, it's very important when taking a strategic approach to board refreshment to identify whether the board's skill sets align with the company's long-term strategic needs.

A board needs to look closely at its company's long-term strategy, map that against the skills around the table, identify potential gaps, and create a matrix. The skills matrix is not a one-and-done task-it's a living document, updated every year against the company's strategy. For example, the board of a bricks-and-mortar retailer planning to establish an ecommerce channel might determine it needs a board member with ecommerce advertising and analytics expertise.

4) Do not let search firms drive the recruitment process

Too often a board's decision to replace a member is triggered by a retirement, an activist, or an institutional shareholder. The result of a passive refreshment process is that search firms wind up driving recruitment by default. A far better practice is for the governance committee to lead the board through it as part of the natural refreshment cycle. That way, the board gets the critical skills it needs and new members understand from the beginning that it's not a lifetime appointment.

When refreshment is driven by a standardized process based on maintaining competitive skill sets, the board isn't caught back on its heels if a board member is suddenly incapacitated or an activist rattles the doors. It's also easier to tell a colleague when it's time for him to surrender his board seat to somebody who has more critically relevant experience.

5) Set guidelines for retirement or term limits
Retirement ages are extending, because people are staying active longer and working longer. Age limit guidelines are an effective way to trigger graceful rotations and maintain director independence. The term is guideline—not mandate—because it's important to retain the ability to waive the age limit as part of governance. For example, at Berkshire Hathaway they'll likely waive any age limit as long as Warren Buffet is sharp.

Europe is leading the way in board term limits; some European countries have already mandated 10-year terms. Institutional shareholders in the U.S. are taking note and beginning to discuss term limits as a method to maintaining director independence. Term limits also keep a board's skill set fresh—but again, the governance committee has to retain the ability, by exception, to waive it. Microsoft isn't going to ask Bill Gates to step down anytime soon.

6) Don't get too comfortable with board colleagues
It's only human that people who serve together on a board will over time become friends, just as coworkers often do. So it becomes awkward to tell a long-time board colleague that they aren't the right person going forward. To make it more difficult, boards lack the hierarchy of a private corporation. Instead they are led by a group of peers, with a lead director or a chairman who should own the board makeup and refreshment topic.

Executing a proactive approach to refreshment eliminates the awkwardness of asking long-time colleagues to leave a board, because transitioning board members off becomes part of a natural, smooth cycle. The expectation is set from the beginning that board appointments are not for life.

7) Measure boardroom diversity using a holistic set of benchmarks
Diversity shouldn't be measured strictly by gender. What boardrooms need is diversity of perspective: gender diversity, ethnic diversity, international diversity, entrepreneurial diversity, and don't forget technical diversity as technology is the biggest disrupter of virtually every business.

Adapted from *Nasdaq Governance Clearinghouse* April 3, 2017.

Diversity on the board may provide customer/market insights and views on the company employees and shareholders, and augment the board's collective process. Having a diverse board is especially useful in difficult situations to help avoid groupthink. Use the annual board assessment to identify gaps in the current skills, hire a search firm to access the broadest pool of talent, and have an objective process. Be sure new directors have a thorough orientation.

Diversity in the Boardroom: Why It's Important and How to Manage It

Experts on leadership and governance have written extensively about diversity in the boardroom—a seemingly inevitable outcome of today's global economy, in addition to the widespread adoption of diversity as a corporate value. Demographic and governance trends aside, there are compelling business reasons for assembling a diverse set of board members. Nominating committees are more frequently taking proactive measures to increase diverse members in their ranks, in ways that will enhance a board's overall value to the company.

The Business Case for Boardroom Diversity

From a business standpoint, why is it valuable to have a diverse set of board members? In my experience serving on the boards of a broad range of companies, I see three primary business arguments for promoting diversity in the boardroom: First, board members from diverse backgrounds can provide direct access to market insight. In many industries, a growing proportion (if not a majority) of purchasing decision makers are women or minorities. Adding females and diverse members greatly enhances a board's ability to understand the perspective of its target audience. Second, diversity supports sound decision making by augmenting the board's collective "processing," which is critical to a well-functioning team.

A strong board of directors brings together differing views from different experience bases. Ideally, it should include perspectives from other industries, as well as functional knowledge of topics ranging from branding and marketing to international trade. A broad set of viewpoints provides collective logic and analytics on how to optimize company opportunities and produce the best outcome. Blended views are particularly important in difficult situations or during a crisis, because

71

they help lessen the chance that a board misses an important issue or viewpoint.

Finally, demographic diversity may allow for better insight into two of a board's main constituents: employees and shareholders. After all, over half of the workforce is female! The investing public is also more heterogeneous than in years past, having grown in the late 1990s to include over 60 million Americans. Investors have continued to grow in numbers and today represent a highly diverse group. Clearly a "diverse" board member must first bring the requisite experience and skills as a public company director. Then his or her "diverse" background and perspective may be an additive advantage.

Determining and Fulfilling Diversity Requirements

How does a board of directors go about determining which skills and perspectives it needs? Best practice for public boards is an annual board assessment review. As part of an annual review to optimize performance, boards assess and map existing skill sets onto a matrix and identify potential gaps. In most cases, a lead director or governance chair leads this activity. The boards of a growing number of large public companies are now beginning to rely on the help of a professional, outside facilitator to map out various perspectives and background skills and conduct the gap analysis. Boards are viewing themselves objectively and seeing if "board renewal" is needed.

The skills and perspectives gap analyses help guide nominating committees when replacing board members who are retiring or rotating out, as they consider requirements. This process helps identify the types of individuals that bring the diversity needed to complement the rest of the board.

Clearly, the next step is to find board members with the targeted backgrounds. The need to build a team of experienced board members who bring judgment is the baseline starting point for considering new director candidates. In terms of best practices, I recommend recruiting board members through an executive search firm. In today's ever-litigious world, an objective, independent process is critical. Use of an executive search firm helps boards avoid the potential charge of cronyism that results from inviting friends and acquaintances to become members. Moreover, an executive search firm makes the board search process more effective by providing access to the broadest pool of talented candidates. Search firms leverage a global candidate pool and bring expertise in identifying and qualifying people with the complementary perspectives required.

Assimilating and Integrating Diverse Board Members

We have already discussed how diverse perspectives and backgrounds strengthen a board of directors through market insight, collective "processing" and problem solving, and more accurate representation of the marketplace, customers, and shareholders. How does a board of directors most effectively integrate a member from a different background into the team?

To be effective, directors have to be well integrated into the organization. A director must understand the company's industry, its competition, and the market. Today boards often conduct regular formal training programs for new directors. The training typically involves meetings with senior management, as well as visits to the company—in some cases, retail stores, manufacturing facilities, etc. As part of the orientation process, boards also encourage new members to spend time with the lead director and/or nominating chair for insight into the team dynamics and its decision-making processes. Having individual meetings with board colleagues provides insight into the board's "institutional memory." This integration process typically takes place during a new director's first quarter.

In summary, bringing diversity into the boardroom benefits shareholders, management and fellow directors by strengthening the oversight team for the enterprise's long-term growth. Done well, the addition of new more diverse directors strengthens the whole board's decision-making and value.

Adapted from Nosal *Inside/Outside* Fall 2006.

Finding the right directors takes work. Get strong buy-in from the board search committee on the ideal specifications for board candidates, and communicate your timeline to the search firm. If you allocate the time and focus, you can build a world-class board.

The Right Fit: Finding a Great Director is Hard Work

Corporate directors should not only be independent, but also smart, ethical, expert, committed, and eager to serve. These days especially, few would dare question such lofty specifications. But if we believe all that, then why do companies still appoint directors who lack one or more of these characteristics? The answer is that finding a great director doesn't just happen—it takes hard work. I know that from personal experience. I serve on three boards, one being Polycom Inc. If that name doesn't set off bells of recognition, just think of the triangle-shaped speakerphones and videoconferencing equipment that one sees in so many conference rooms today. Polycom, a $500 million NASDAQ corporation based in Pleasanton, California, is the leader in both of these markets—it owns for instance, 94 percent of the world market in speakerphones among companies that use them.

But a year ago, we estimated that we had tapped only 8 percent of the market—92 percent of companies don't use speakerphones. If we wanted Polycom to become a multi-billion-dollar company—and we certainly did, and do—we outside directors realized that we could not achieve that goal with the makeup of our existing board. Not that the five of us were untalented or uncommitted to the task. The problem was that we, and Polycom's two inside directors, all came from technical backgrounds. If we were to successfully enter the consumer market, our board needed expertise in branding and in expanding into retail channels.

Even more than expertise, we wanted to add directors who had the time to mentor our CEO in order to take Polycom to the next level. Who better to meet this challenge than a recently retired CEO! Not only would he have the time for mentoring, his knowledge of management and network of contacts would be current.

Our specifications then were clear-cut: a recently retired CEO of a large public company who had a background in branding and retailing—and who could help our CEO scale the business. It's one thing to set forth specifications, however, and quite another to fill them. That task fell to me as chairman of Polycom's nominating and governance committee.

The board felt that it needed an executive search firm to get the best possible prospects into the pipeline and I asked for directors' recommendations. We put together a panel of five firms and quickly narrowed it to two: Christian & Timbers and Korn/Ferry International. After interviewing both firms, I recommended Korn/Ferry to the board. Both were excellent, but I felt that Christian & Timbers' strength was in technology, and we weren't looking for technology. I felt Korn/Ferry was more mainstream with a Fortune 1000 list of clients who were apt to have the retail and branding expertise that we were seeking.

I created a timeline for the search and told Korn/Ferry that we expected to see a list of candidates within two weeks. Certainly that was a tight time frame, but I've found that if you communicate your expectations and display your commitment by making yourself available to review and consider recommendations, then you can get a search firm to perform quickly. I've found firms' responsiveness to be directly related to the search committee's level of engagement.

In two weeks' time, Korn/Ferry came up with a list of 22 candidates who fit our specifications, and we on the nominating committee added candidates of our own. That combined list of 35 people was circulated to the full board and subsequently winnowed back down to 22; some of those had been screened as to their interest in serving on a board, some not.

I then asked the directors to rank the 22, so we could let Korn/Ferry know whom we were most interested in. At this point, we had detailed résumés to compare against our specifications, but it was still like herding cats to get my board to do it. We finally cut down the list to 12 and also refined our requirements by adding another: that the candidate have a strong operating background with an emphasis on marketing and market entry. So, for example, a CEO of a large retail company who had come up through the ranks as a CFO would be less desirable than a CEO who had come up through marketing. After a further winnowing and ranking process, we reduced the 12 candidates to five.

Korn/Ferry then took our short list and contacted each of the five to determine their interest and availability in serving on a board. With five affirmatives, I interviewed each of the candidates. Their reactions, I found, were uniformly positive. They weren't necessarily familiar with the name Polycom, but once I mentioned speakerphones, everyone knew what I meant. The fact that they didn't immediately recognize the name, I pointed out, was part of the company's problem—that its brand was not widely known—and part of the reason why we were considering them for a director's position.

Apart from its low visibility, Polycom was in a strong position, with 19 quarters of profitability and a vigorous commitment to best practices in governance. This was most emphatically not, I pointed out to the board candidates, a messed-up company that needed shoveling out. We also offered an attractive compensation package; an annual fee of $50,000, along with an annual "refresh" grant of $25,000 and an initial stock option of 60,000 shares over a four-year vest.

The candidates responded positively. While not from the technology sector, they all realized that technology was the future and something they wanted to be a part of. So they were drawn to the possibility of involvement with a prestigious technology company.

After talking with the five candidates and conveying my impressions to the nominating committee, we reduced the number from five to two: Durk Jager, 59, the former chairman and CEO of Procter & Gamble, and Tom Stemberg, 52, the founder and former CEO of Staples. In interviews, we found Jager to be extremely thoughtful and analytical, with a strong view of management and succession planning as well as an incredible understanding of branding. Stemberg had sharp insights into operational issues: how a corporation should think about entering a retail channel and what the inflection points are in growing a business.

Both men then met with the entire board, who wanted to hear from them directly about whether what we thought was important was also important to them. If they told us, for example, that Polycom offered too few products, we would have said that we thought we offered too many already—the issue is how we brand them. If they told us that we needed more internal financial controls, we would have responded, "We feel we're great at this—why do you see it as an issue?" We also wanted to hear about their thought processes. Yes, as a company we knew that we needed to be more process- and strategy-oriented, but it would be a bad match for us if we brought aboard a McKinsey-type, long-range-only thinker.

In our talks, both Jager and Stemberg asked us good, thought-provoking questions, to draw us out on whether the future was a bright as we believed it to be, whether the company's technology was well-thought-out from a quality point of view, whether the financial reputation of the company was as good as it appeared, and so on. Later, we invited them to company headquarters to meet with the CEO, CFO, and selected division leaders. Right from the beginning of our search, we had stipulated that the CEO would have veto power over the prospective board members if he had an "allergic" reaction to them (although he had no additional power, except as one among seven board members to say who should be on the slate from which the two were finally chosen).

Late last year, we voted to add Jager and Stemberg to the Polycom board. We're pleased with the way the process worked out, but as I said earlier, it was a *process* rather than something that just happened. The selection and hiring required hard work by every member of the board and some four months, a period over which the search ate up some 40 percent of my time. Was it worth the effort? Absolutely.

Adapted from *Across the Board* July/August 2003.

How to Win in the Digital Revolution

We are in the throes of a digital industrial revolution, and every company must contend with the rapid pace of change. In this environment of innovation and upheaval, companies cannot merely defend their products against this newest wave of competitors. Instead, they must learn how disrupt themselves.

But in this day and age, even the concept of a product is in flux. The customer experience has become more important than products in a traditional sense of the term. But who is the customer, and how are they engaging with the 21st-century marketplace— and why are certain companies already ahead of the curve in answering these questions?

Take Out the Friction

The new business models exemplified by Apple Pay and Uber Technologies have proven that when you remove transaction friction— i.e., simplify the process of trading goods and services—you delight users and can rapidly convert huge chunks of the market at unimaginable speed.

Look at how quickly consumers embraced Uber—now a $10 billion company—because it removed the steps of payment and tipping from the taxi experience. Apple Pay similarly pared down the purchasing process: you pull out your phone and place your finger on the pay button. That's it—no fumbling with a wallet, personal identification numbers, or signing receipts.

Some large, well-established companies like The Walt Disney Co. understand this need to remove friction. In 2013, the company rolled out MagicBand, a digitally enhanced bracelet that allows the wearer to enter Disney theme parks, unlock their Disney resort hotel room, buy food and merchandise, and access passes to theme park experiences. Enterprises need to examine how customers conduct transactions, map the entire customer journey, and uncover the places where friction can—and should— be taken out of the system.

For these companies, reducing friction can be extraordinarily difficult. These enterprises likely have legacy information technology systems that were designed without today's digital marketplace in mind. These systems must be re-orchestrated to integrate with mobile devices, cloud computing, and front-end, customer-friendly software experiences.

The other hard part of reducing friction is overhauling an organization's well-ingrained work flows. Cross-functional teams of senior executives must be empowered if these changes are to happen. Your chief information officer now needs to be your Chief Information Officer.

Finding Clarity
The line between marketing and engineering is becoming less defined—and that's a good thing. Merging these disciplines will destroy silos and make product teams more nimble and consumer-insight driven.

Digital marketing using big data analytics will require investment in experiment-driven marketing and research, either through building internal capabilities or partnering with specialists. This kind of work will demand executive-level acceptance of (small) failures as part of uncovering scalable opportunities. A culture of experimentation will yield fast wins or fast fails through quick proof of concepts.

Blurring borders
The ease of e-commerce continues to accelerate by reducing friction. This also results in greater integration of web, app, and e-commerce platforms. Marketplaces integrate application interfaces from other companies so consumers will visit one marketplace to book all the services they need. For example, using the United Airlines app, you can book a flight and an Uber ride to get you to and from the airport.

Social media platforms are already tying e-commerce features into their networks, from Instagram's "Shop Now" to Pinterest's "Buyable Pins." This practice will be increasingly used in the coming years. Ask yourself how to apply this practice to your business-to-business or business-to-consumer strategies.

Traditional marketing has held that people don't shop on social media, but as mobile technologies, social media, and e-commerce become more integrated, the possibilities open up to hit the right combination of buying and browsing buttons to capture this "quick digital" revenue.

The sharing economy. Globally, the sharing economy's size was roughly $15 billion in 2014, and it's projected to reach $335 billion by 2025. Far from a fad, this is the new way of doing business. In addition to examples like Uber and Airbnb, look at TaskRabbit, an online, mobile-optimized marketplace that matches local freelance labor with demand, allowing consumers to find immediate help with everyday tasks such as cleaning, moving, and delivery. This company has created affordable solutions for cash-conscious consumers and offers unique income streams for people needing extra money or flexible work schedules.

The sharing economy's story doesn't end with taxis, vacation rentals, and freelancers. As consumers share and recycle their belongings, overall product demand might decrease. Companies will compete with millions of consumers willing to rent the same product for a fraction of the cost.

The gig economy

Just as a musician plays temporary engagements, companies going forward won't hire head count directly; they'll outsource it through, for example, companies like GlobalLogic, a digital product development services provider. According to a 2015 Pew Research Center study, the Millennial generation has the greatest representation in the American workforce: 53.5 million people, or approximately one in three workers. And according to PwC global survey of some 4,300 college graduates, this generation greatly values training and development programs, competitive pay, and flexible hours. As a result, employment will fluctuate radically as a larger portion of the employee base seeks jobs that offer more flexible arrangements.

Profit for purpose

Millennials now drive a significant amount of our economy. They're active, informed, and building discretionary income. In 2015, consumers demanded more authenticity and transparency from the brands they used. Without a clear purpose and high ethical standards, companies will find themselves floundering.

How incumbents experience change. Long-lived "incumbent" companies generally experience disruptions to their business model very slowly at first; then, when it's too late, they can't recover. For example, it took Blockbuster six years to realize that Netflix was a threat, but by that point it was too late to correct course.

Traditional market intermediaries are also losing their relevance. Look at the travel agent industry, where revenue collapsed from $160 billion to less than $40 billion between 2000 and 2014, but during the same period online hotel revenue soared from $10 billion to $130 billion.

What Does This Teach Us?

These new innovators get traction because they create a frictionless, efficient experience that improves our lives. They have also proven themselves adaptable to changing demographics and market trends.

Incumbents currently hold the power because they own customer relationships, brands, intellectual property, and strong financials. There are large companies that have innovated and adopted new models that embrace collaborative efforts with other companies.

We must learn from those that haven't innovated—such as Polaroid, Borders, Blockbuster, and Circuit City. The causes and indicators of these companies' failures can be applied to our own companies. Here's how to win:

Create a culture of external orientation. Focus on your customers' needs and desires first, then build a set of tactics and strategy around that customer profile.

Take the best ideas, test them, learn from the results, and repeat that process. Tolerate failure. Use data-driven decision making. Invest in connectivity, create resonant content, and be bold. Let go of your past.

Succeed in the future

Companies must have a program to iterate until they find new ways to innovate. Ultimately, if you don't disrupt your business, a competitor will.

Your company will become irrelevant if you are not actively observing and listening to your customers—"business as usual" no longer exists. If you try to follow a trend in half-step or react to behavior, you are not sufficiently thinking in terms that will ensure the long-term success of your company. To remain relevant, plan to compete for the future by

being proactive and adaptive, and creating meaningful consumer experiences.

Adapted From *NACDonline.org* July/August 2016.

In this brief article, I highlight the pros and cons of using a recruiter to build a board. When using recruiters, make sure they look for the more subjective qualities needed in a corporate director. Recruiters can bring an objective process with a well-defined specification, profile and network of candidates, but the board must not lose focus on what makes a great director: engaged business judgment to help anticipate risks and help balance long- and short-term decisions for the shareholders.

Recruiters: Helpful Facilitators vs. (Un)intentional Gatekeepers

Recruiters definitely are an important, objective part of the nominating and governance committee process. They help craft a crisp, clear specification and skill set profile. They have a wide network and can bring in and introduce to the board new, talented, prospective directors. Additionally, recruiters can provide a decision framework for the nominating committee to review prospective new colleagues by defining a matrix of different skills each potential new director brings.

Alternatively, on the negative side, recruiters (unless instructed by the nominating committee) may be too fixated on quantitative skill matrix "checkboxes" and miss the true essence of what makes a great director. The essence of being a great director is bringing valuable business judgment to anticipate the company's future risks, and helping management balance short- and long-term goals to build a resilient enterprise for the shareholders.

Box checking of skills will capture quantifiable experiences, such as:

— financial expert for audit committee,
— diversity candidate,
— industry domain expertise,
— sitting CEO.
—

But a skills matrix may miss the most important aspects of understanding if a candidate can truly be valuable through his or her understanding of:

— the company's business,
— its opportunities,
— its competitive market dynamics,

83

— its growth challenges.

Other qualitative attributes that make for a truly high-value-add director include:

— business judgment,
— business experience to understand the issues the company faces,
— being deeply versed in the trade-offs of organic vs. inorganic growth,
— ability to add valuable insight to help management maximize the company's execution in the market,
— ability to mentor the CEO and encourage systems to develop the leadership team.

Many search firms miss these qualitative aspects. Ultimately, the nominating committee must balance the checklist of quantitative skills matrix that the search firm will present against the qualitative and deeply essential attributes of business experience and business judgment that combine to make a prospective highly valuable addition to the board.

Adapted from *Directors & Boards* Second Quarter 2013.

Inside The Boardroom with Betsy Atkins Q3 2016

"Negotiating difficult boardroom situations is something veteran Director Betsy Atkins knows a thing or two about, and she's got plenty of battle scars to prove it. In 2003, for example, during a brief stint as a director of HealthSouth, she chaired a special litigation committee to investigate massive accounting fraud charges levied against the company.

More recently, as a director at Wix, Atkins and the board had to make a painful, but ultimately correct, decision to pay a ransom after a serious DDoS cyberattack locked up the company's servers. In light of her broad governance experience serving on the boards of more than 20 public companies, Atkins often receives inquiries from fellow directors asking for advice— something we thought was worth sharing with our readers.

Therefore, in the spirit of "Dear Abby," we're inviting you to submit questions to "Ask Betsy" about your toughest boardroom dilemmas. Chances are, she's been in the same trenches as you and has sage advice to share."

Dear Betsy,

Our CEO for the last 12 years is a member of the founding family that started our company 32 years ago.

It's become obvious to the board that he is an impediment to the growth that we feel is necessary to move forward, and we have spoken in executive session about how to plan for his leadership transition. Unfortunately, the CEO has made it clear he does not wish to discuss his own succession plan. What can we do?

Betsy: CEO succession is consistently the most sensitive subject, and a significant majority of CEOs are very resistant to addressing the succession topic. The key duty of care and duty of loyalty obligation of all public directors is to ensure leadership continuity. Doing so implies an obligation to ensure the right leader is in place for the company's future. An effective way to address succession is to first reach consensus and alignment in an executive session led by the nonexec chair or lead director on what the ideal profile is for the future leader, identifying the skills, experiences, attributes, and characteristics needed for the coming five years. By creating a nonemotional profile, the directors will reach a common view. It is critical to have the board aligned and totally bought in to successfully drive change.

The next step is to put succession on the agenda as a consistent topic for the coming four board meetings. Expect the first meeting to be the most awkward, with some degree of bad behavior by the current CEO. Expect the second meeting to be only slightly less awkward with more bad behavior and some of the directors beginning to equivocate, since it's likely the CEO will backchannel to allies on the board. Stay the course.

By the third meeting, things should start to cohere a bit, and by the fourth meeting, there should be acceptance and alignment that a change is needed. The third step is to create a formal search committee typically made up of two or three committee chairs, plus the lead independent or nonexec chair. And the final step is to engage an outside executive search firm to conduct a review of the current CEO and internal successors, as well as the external marketplace.

–B

Dear Betsy,

Our board struggles with what our role ought to be with regard to the corporate strategy, though we've always heard "fingers out, noses in." In your experience, how much involvement should a board have in setting strategy?

Betsy: This is a very tricky and important question. At a high level, the board reviews and approves the strategy. A best practice is an annual, multiday board meeting devoted to strategy. Board members have oversight responsibility for strategy and may contribute input. The critical delineation is that management owns, operates, and implements strategy.

The board is not an operating group. The board is an oversight group operating on behalf of the shareholders to make sure the strategy is robust for both the short term and, importantly, the longer term. Balancing the pressures of short-term quarterly performance against the need to be competitive and strong for the long term where capital investments are required is one of the key discussion items to address annually.

Often, part of a quarterly board meeting relates back to the annual strategy execution with presentations on competitive market dynamics, and any potential acquisition that supports the strategic goals. A clear strategy with a well understood framework will allow the board to understand the company's goals and measure the success of the company's strategy.

-B

Dear Betsy,

How important is it for board members to visit the company and observe operations and managers on a regular basis?

Betsy: We've debated whether or not to institute this on a regular basis. Board members need access to the senior leadership team. One of the most important insights is to understand the morale of the company and whether senior leaders are encouraged to contribute, question, and challenge, or is it a command and control environment?

Directors cannot get this insight unless they have access; a CEO that discourages access presents a big red flag.

Visiting operations is extremely valuable; it is motivating for the company's leadership team to see the directors' interest. It is highly valuable for the directors to get a deeper understanding of the company's business and competitive dynamics through these interactions. A best practice that is evolving is for directors to visit the company's operations annually. Additionally, new director "on boarding" often includes one-on-one time with the senior leaders and exposure on site to the operations.

-B

Dear Betsy,

I am the audit committee chairman on the board of an $800 million health care company and cybersecurity is a huge concern. What do you recommend as a best practice for overseeing the cyber risk arena? Right now we are trying to get a handle on oversight within our full board meetings, but would you recommend setting up a special committee for that purpose?

Betsy: Cyber risk is certainly a huge priority for companies in the health care arena. There is special liability around protecting patient identity as well as the high-value intellectual property associated with new drug development. Creating a separate committee for cyber would typically not be necessary. Normally, cyber oversight would be handled by the audit committee as part of an enterprise risk framework review. Cyber is sometimes considered the next step following the IT disaster recovery planning that the audit committee oversees. A more innovative approach to consider would be to have a technology committee that looks forward to anticipate risks. The type of forward-looking risks to consider would be new market competitors, business models that could impact and disintermediate your core business, i.e., ecommerce giants like Amazon and Alibaba, or marketplace business models like Airbnb, Uber, eBay, or other competitive market risks. As part of the forward-looking risk landscape, cyber oversight would reside in a tech committee.

–B

Adapted from *Corporate Board Member* Third Quarter 2016.

Inside the Boardroom with Betsy Atkins Q1 2017

"There's often no better source of information than a person who has stood in your shoes. So in that spirit, consummate boardroom insider Betsy Atkins returns with responses to several of our readers' questions. This quarter, she tackles issues related to board composition and refreshment, how to handle disruption and innovation, dividing and conquering board committee work, and the importance of board diversity."

Dear Betsy,

Our board is having a hard time with the whole concept of board refreshment. About half of our board is made up on members who have been on the board for more than 10 years. Some of us think that collective experience is a valuable asset and are unwilling to consider a board tenure policy. Others (the younger directors) believe that boards today should definitely have tenure policy that limits the time served. What are your thoughts?

Betsy: Board refreshment is an emotionally charged subject and one that is taking hold among boardrooms globally. A growing number of countries in Europe, for example, are embracing guidelines that recommend tenures between nine and 12 years as a best practice and many European boards have defined term limits. While there is value in the institutional memory around the board table, it is important to augment the board with new perspectives, especially since the rate of change corporations face in the competitive marketplace has increased geometrically. I think the best way to thread the needle is to put in a term limit, but allow the governance committee to make an exception just as the governance committee has the same authority to grant an exception where needed, just as the governance committee has the same authority to grant an exception on retirement age policies and auto resignations that are triggered by a role change for board members. This way your board has a mechanism for renewing itself, but has some flexibility to keep its most exceptional members. This is also a proactive way to demonstrate to shareholders that your board is not sitting idly by without addressing the topic.

Dear Betsy,

I sit on the board of a $500 million financial outsourcing firm. We often have discussions about the risk of disruptive innovations and what they will mean to the growth of our company. In your view, how often should we be talking about topics like this? Once a year? More often? How can we address disruption risk in an organized manner?

Betsy: I believe that it is time for boards to consider either adding a strategy/technology committee or augmenting the scope of one of the current standing committees to have a specific mandate to regularly review the company's strategy through the lens of innovative business models like "the marketplace model" like eBay, VRBO, Uber. The committee could review the use of software enablement, cyber, mobile, social, AI, analytics, and other major themes, and how the company is using technology to either take costs out or more deeply engage with its customers since these innovations are definitely disrupting businesses. Additionally, the committee could more deeply understand the company's future development roadmap for products and services with an eye to the external competitive landscape. I would suggest that this tech/strategy oversight be performed regularly, i.e., as part of a quarterly committee review.

Dear Betsy,

It's important to our board that each member be grounded in as many important governance areas as possible and so we've started asking members to sit in and listen to committee meetings where they are not an active member. Some directors are beginning to grumble that this is asking too much of their time, and feel additional compensation should, at a minimum be afforded. Have you had experience with this and could you offer any recommendations?

Betsy: I recommend that you have an environment that is open and allows members to sit in on other committees where there is an interest and desire. I think you go too far in asking members to listen in on all of the committees. The reason I do not support this is that it undermines the primary responsibility of the committee if non committee members are sitting in because … inevitably non committee members opine and participate. Expecting board members to sit mutely on a committee and not engage is not realistic in my view. Additionally, the purpose of having committees is for the board to be efficient and allow a subset of the board to be deeply engaged and "own" an important responsibility on behalf of the whole board and report back out. I think your colleagues are right to grumble.

Dear Betsy,

There is considerable discussion about diversity among directors. How does a board make sure that diverse members are not regarded as placeholders but seen as important contributors to the board, equal in value and importance to all other directors?

Betsy: Strong boards are built upon a diversity of experience, viewpoints, and perspectives.

Diversity comes in a range of backgrounds: minorities, gender diversity, and, critically, diversity of thought. Gender diversity is currently being mandated in the EU; for example, Harvard Business Review's recent article cites mandatory quotas of 25% to 40% for female board member representation in Germany, France, Belgium, Iceland, and Italy, with a recommended female diversity target of 25% for the UK. America's free market has not embraced government mandates, but we have seen an increase to 18.7% gender diversity in the S&P 500 (19.7% in the Fortune 500). Institutional shareholders are urging more diversity, thus boards must be able to communicate clearly how they are addressing diversity of thought and perspective and may want to consider proactively adding gender and minority diversity as part of their profile for board refreshment. However, it is essential to bring on qualified members to avoid the label of "placeholders."

Adapted from *Corporate Board Member* First Quarter 2017.

The Future of Boards: Framing Your Personal Brand for Board Opportunities

Private and public companies are starting to crystallize and articulate a new model for what they want from directors and advisors. Because companies are experiencing change at an accelerated rate and are struggling to keep up, CEOs and the executive team are more frequently turning to their board members for their expertise to help solve issues quickly and help drive strategies for long-term growth and success.

There is an opportunity as a perspective advisor/director to own and take control of the language and positioning for the future of the boards and define the value and impact that board members bring to the table. To be an impactful board member, you need to bring certain qualitative attributes and quantitative skills to the boardroom.

Qualitatives Attributes for Highly Engaged Board Members

The qualitative attributes companies look for in their board members are headlined by a high level of engagement. Companies expect more from their board members than just showing up for quarterly board meetings. They expect advisors/directors to be in touch with the CEO on a regular basis by phone and email between meetings. This high level of engagement is critical—companies need advisors/directors who will spend their mental calories to devise ways they can move the business forward, anticipate competitive dynamics and solve issues. They want director who are willing to leverage their network and share their contact list to facilitate impactful introductions. Board members need to become a differentiator and a "competitive asset." Directors/Advisors should be an accelerant for the business.

The days of showing up for a meeting having read your board materials and sharing a few sage opinions on strategy are over. Companies are looking for directors that engage in a meaningful, measureable ways. If you take the step of identifying the quantifiable things you can deliver, you will stand out. You'll also sharpen your thinking by creating a specific list of ways you can contribute to the business.

Quantitative Attributes for Results-driven Board Members

In terms of quantitative attributes, companies want to see specific examples for how you will help grow and accelerate their business. At this point in your career, you are a senior and accomplished executive who has likely had an extraordinary amount of varied and valuable experiences. Pull from your own "menu" of experiences and tailor them to a crisply defined set of "projects/deliverables" that would move the company forward in differentiated way—for example; facilitating the capture of revenue, hosting a meeting that results in closing new sales, giving clear insights to help solve a problem, or making connections and introductions that will lead to a specific mutually discussed and agreed useful outcome for the company.

Companies especially look for advisors/directors who brings specific vertical industry knowledge. For example, if the business is in the health care industry, a director with knowledge in the health care systems is highly desirable. A director who brings specific functional domain knowledge to augment strengths around the table is also valuable. This could include market knowledge, product innovation, supply chain, global expansion, branding, or go-to-market strategies.

Positioning Yourself for Board Opportunities
Be very specific in how you market and position yourself for board opportunities. General "corporate speak" gets lost. Think about what you bring qualitatively that a board would consider "a must have," and then map the quantitative strengths that you can contribute toward accelerating the company. Identify what you would do in a concrete way that helps the company do at least one of the following: grow top line revenue, be unique against competitors, drive efficiency, or increase profit etc. These themes will resonate with the decision maker who will determine if you are the right fit.

Boards go through an informal "get to know you" process as they interview candidates. So, do your homework—delve into the company and learn about the business, the competition, and the business model. Map out your accomplishments and experiences in a way that it is directly relevant and compelling to the company. Create specific, short, crisp talking points about yourself and the value you bring. (I recommend talking points to be no longer than a tweet in length.)

Apply this specific tailored response approach when you write your resume as well. A general resume is a good starting point. Create a library of specifically tailored versions of your resume for each company you are approaching. Framing your own personal brand and tailoring it to a particular board opportunity will help position you for the right opportunity.

Change is coming. Companies are forming boards that are focused on the future of their business, and play a highly active role in driving a growth strategy for long-term success. These highly engaged, results-driven boards are seen by CEOs as a competitive advantage. They are constantly thinking about the business and how the company is positioned for its markets and competition to further long-term success. By defining your position on a board early articulating and positioning the value and impact that you bring to a company's success, you can play a part in redefining the role of future boards.

Adapted from *ExecRanks Quarterly* Spring 2017.

CHAPTER 5: BOARD RISKS

Information governance as an oversight item for boards doing complete risk management requires document retention, current e-discovery indexing, and a policy that delineates what must be retained and what can be deleted. Policies must be clearly communicated, trained, and complied with to avoid surprise costs and big risks.

Traditional board oversight needs to be augmented by a director with "digital DNA" who knows ecommerce, mobile, social, marketing, automation, etc. Companies die because their strategy gets stale and they don't recognize the market changes. Just as boards learned they needed a financial expert, now they need a director with digital expertise as well.

The Digital Director

In the last millennium, directors knew they had an affirmative duty to watch over a corporation's finances and business decisions for the longevity and health of the enterprise. According to author Jim Collins, *Good to Great*, 40 percent of all corporations have a life span of only 20 years. Why do these companies die? It's because their strategy gets stale and non competitive. Look at Border's—Amazon made them obsolete.

The major megatrends of E-commerce, Mobile Enablement, Social Media, and Marketing Automation have changed how companies acquire customers; analyze and gain insight into customer behavior and product preference; and retain loyal customers by creating brand advocates. This is essential to be a viable company.

This millennium's board must have some digital directors that have social/mobile/digital "DNA." Today's boards need deep knowledge and understanding of these digital/social/e-commerce and mobile megatrends and how they will impact, influence, and possibly disintermediate large portions of business at the companies they serve.

Without a deep experience and understanding of E-commerce, Mobile, Social Media, and Marketing Automation, boards lack an essential frame of reference. This is a serious myopia that may impact their ability to perform valuable oversight on a company's strategy and investment.

A couple of simple examples will illuminate this. At Schneider, the $35B electrical equipment and energy efficiency company (competing with Honeywell, Siemens, etc.) E-commerce is a gigantic megatrend that will have enormous impact. Traditional distribution channels—selling electrical components, circuit breakers, lighting control equipment to national distributors such as Graybar and Grainger—are threatened by Amazon, which sells directly to the same consumer and electrical contractors. How should Schneider address this E-commerce megatrend that threatens to disintermediate their distribution channel? A board cannot opine with knowledge on this critical strategic decision unless some directors have direct knowledge and current experience, and expertise in E-commerce.

There were 2.4 billion Internet users in 2012, with an 8 percent year-on-year growth. The mobile trend toward smartphones has huge upside. Currently only 17 percent of mobile phone users are utilizing smartphones. Global mobile phone Internet usage has surged from 2 percent of total Internet traffic to 10 percent of the total in the last four years. This represents a tectonic shift in the way consumers buy products and services. Chico's, the $3B specialty retailer on whose board I serve, has embraced mobile shopping, mobile coupons and the capture of mobile sentiment via ratings and reviews. iPad growth is three times iPhone growth and we know Chico's shoppers shop via their iPad. They are typical North America consumers: multichannel shoppers! Chico's has invested successfully in their e-commerce platform; our board embraces the importance of the social media/marketing automation and mobile megatrends and has enacted them to make the Chico's brand relevant at their brick and mortar stores as well as on the web.

Boards need directors who bring "digital DNA" to the boardroom. Directors who are informed, engaged, knowledgeable, and current on these major trends can provide appropriate board oversight both to ensure companies are investing strategically, as well as to understand and appreciate the significance and key competitive importance of major corporate investments supporting the megathemes: E-commerce, Mobile, Social Media, and Marketing Automation. This is as valuable a skill set as audit committee members with Sarbanes-Oxley 404 expertise.

I'm confident boards will recognize and increase their pace of adding Digital DNA directors to ensure their corporations thrive beyond the statistical mortality rates. More companies flatline because they don't continuously innovate and lead their category. The risk is they become smaller in their vision and incremental in their approach to embracing these huge technology and societal mega trends. Wake up and add some Digital DNA to your boardroom today!

First published in this volume.

Big Data and the Board

Business operations today collect enormous amounts of data, but the idea of using technology to gather, crunch, and analyze this data in new ways for strategic advantage is fairly new. In a world where every business is a technology business, corporate boards have a duty to bring into the boardroom fresh ideas, outside concepts and perspectives, and early warnings of coming change. And when it comes to Big Data simply asking, "So what are we doing with it?" at the next board meeting is not enough. That's the sort of thing directors do just to let everyone know they're familiar with the latest buzzword (and awake).

Instead, I suggest that smart directors ask both strategic and tactical questions that tie in with the board's oversight duties:

How have we budgeted for the use of Big Data analytics, and what are future budget plans?
Effective commitment to data analytics requires investment deep enough to make it a strategic imperative, and also long term enough to stay relevant. This is a field with fast-moving technology, standards and goals. Ask about strategic plans over the next few years.

How does our use of Big Data tie in with overall strategic plans?
Is the data used to drive decisions, or just to back up someone's intuition? To improve efficiency, and if so, in what area—marketing, manufacturing, logistics? To lessen risk (and if so which ones, and how)? Even an investment as something as valuable as Big Data analytics is wasteful if it doesn't deliver solid benefits.

Innovative boards will use data analytics not just to draw conclusions based on past results, but also to derive good insights for future decision making. The role of data analytics is to deliver insights to back up intuition, and also empower the board to ask bold questions. The great mathematician John Tukey observed: "It's more important to get an approximate answer to the right question, than to get a precise answer to the wrong question."

There are many new examples of companies using Big Data to ask "the right questions." A well-known e-commerce firm uses its Big Data teams to predict within one percent the chargebacks that will result from fraud on their website. Targeted use of data analytics not only helps this company protect their merchants from fraud, but also helps it manage costs and allocate their budgets wisely for the future.

Another area that Big Data Analytics can be used is in the area of finding the right mix of budgeting on customer acquisition versus customer retention. According to Gartner, 80% of a company's future revenue will come from 20% of existing customers. Bain and Company research shows that a mere 5% increase in customer retention boosts profitability by 75%. It's generally accepted that it's five times more expensive to acquire a new customer than to retain an existing one.

An innovative organization will apply new technologies such as Big Data analytics comprehensively and cohesively across all customer facing channels (mobile, Web, email, or physical store), and up and down the supply chain. Innovative boards will set up dashboards to show precisely where strategy meets tactics. Comprehensive, innovative dashboards can ensure that the board's mandated strategy is instantly applied, market conditions and demands are appropriately reflected, and customer needs are best served, all with smart board oversight of execution.

We are entering a brave new world where technological tools are now available for boards to deliver optimal value to shareholders—and Big Data should be high on any board's agenda.

Adapted from *The Wall Street Journal–CIO Journal*, Apr16, 2015.

Why Today's Boards Need Tech Savvy: (and Why It Still Isn't Enough)

How is your board addressing technology? Strategic thinking is what is needed to use technology as a tool to drive your company's business forward.

As a member of four corporate boards and a venture investor with a strong interest in good governance, I encounter lots of clichés about the "changing role of the board of directors" today. One popular observation is that technology is radically changing how everyone does business, and that smart boards need to be on top of the issue. Very true—but that's not nearly enough.

Governance clichés won't deliver the smart board oversight needed for today's fast-moving issues like cybersecurity, data analytics, social media/ad tech marketing, and mobile technology—much less for anticipating the new tech challenges and opportunities flooding in at increasing velocity. Good corporate governance demands boardroom talent, structures, information, and drive to be effective. This means that if your company is going to be ready for the digital age, your board must be willing to reshape itself for this oversight task.

So far, boards have been pretty halfhearted about this structural shift. A survey by the NACD found 40% of US public company board members feel they receive too little info on tech challenges facing the company. More interesting, barely 5% of these boards have a dedicated technology committee.

How does today's best-practice board build technology oversight into its DNA? I've served on the boards of a number of firms with strong tech elements and personally know board members of major Fortune 500 companies with tech committees. Pooling our experiences with governing technology, here are some ideas.

Realize that tech is a vital area of governance oversight
Ask business leaders today what their top five priorities are and "digitalization" is inevitably near the top. "Technological advances are defining and shaping our globally connected economy and fueling new growth opportunities for businesses," says Maggie Wilderotter, executive

chairman of Frontier Communications. But where does digitalization—big data and analytics technology, mobile, social media, etc.—fit on your board agenda? When was it last a topic of strategic board discussion?

Consider a board technology committee... but first, consider the role it should play

Even at companies with a board tech committee, it's rarely a pure "technology" committee. American Express has an Innovation and Technology committee. At FedEx it's an Information Technology Oversight committee. Don't let the committee get bogged down in IT reports or backward-looking forensic disaster recovery plans. Instead, focus on how to make smart, strategic use of new and coming technology. "Not every board needs a committee to do this, but the subject matter needs to be routinely brought to the board's attention," says Robert "Steve" Miller Jr., former executive officer of Hawker Beechcraft (now Beechcraft Corp.) and currently nonexecutive chairman at American International Group, as well as a number of other boards.

Yet other business leaders I spoke to are bullish on the need for a committee tightly focused on tech itself. Ted Leonsis, venture capitalist and former top AOL exec, finds a "dedicated technology committee allows for a fresh perspective and a diverse set of thinking from industry experts."

Make this committee your board's forward-looking fiduciary

Current board committees have been shaped by regulatory demands—they're in business to assure compliance and to review yesterday's information. But boards today need a built-in voice that looks *ahead* rather than *behind*.

I've found that a technology discussion is a natural fit with a board's strategic and innovation duties and can kick in fresh thinking from the very top. The tech committee charter should assign it to look at new business models (such as ecommerce), competitive dynamics, and how technology can be exploited for the future.

Here's an example. A $3 billion retail company asked me to join its board to bring in some digital know-how. The company was tech savvy but hesitant to embrace ecommerce because management thought any dollar earned online was one lost by its bricks-and-mortar retailers. It took some boardroom prodding, but eventually this retailer invested in social

101

media and mobile engagement, plus a robust ecommerce platform. Result—the company found the move to be very profitable and a source of net new customers.

This points to one of the most surprising, but vital aspects of the new board tech committee—*tech is not the ultimate point of the committee, but rather an important tool in its forward-looking mandate.* Top business leader Gary Reiner heads the board tech committee at Citi, and notes "since technology is a big part of the company's cost structure, [we] see if there are ways to take advantage of new technology and better practices to reduce the cost and still get the same (or better) productivity." He finds tech is not the "end" for board focus at Citi, but a tool for "enabling faster, simpler, lower cost ways to interact with customers and new business models."

Who should serve on a board tech committee?
No, you shouldn't automatically seek techies for this committee. Focus on breadth of experience. A proven top executive with solid exposure to cyber tech, social and mobile media, big data analytics, and ecommerce brings both the business *and* the technology savvy demanded. A tech industry leader, a corporate CIO, or consulting firm member who specializes in tech are a few of the talent pools to explore. Mixing deep technology expertise with a former or current CIO, chief marketing officer, or business development strategist on the committee may cover these bases. Be willing to look outside your comfortable board circles for skill. "Boards typically have senior folks as members, few of whom are schooled in info tech," notes Steve Miller.

How should a board tech committee function?
In many ways, it's just another committee of the board. It should meet around four times yearly, with three or four members as described above. But I'd include some crucial differences. While most information that boards receive is *inward* facing (company reports, financials, filings, etc.), give the tech committee an *outward* focus. Members should review industry and analyst reports on the company and its sector (not just stock analyst reports). Focus on maximizing your markets, your margins, and potential growth areas. Identify where the company should lead versus its competitors (i.e., do you want to lead in ecommerce or use data analytics to drive customer intimacy?) The committee then becomes the board's "what if?" and "why not?" advocate. It voices technology risk

issues such as cybercrime and hacking, but also addresses risks the company business model could overlook, causing the company to lose out by missing new tech opportunities, such as using mobile enablement or big data to drive new analytic insights and engagement.

A board technology committee fills a vital need in the modern boardroom. It brings focused knowledge of technology to address the strategy and innovation oversight that is too often squeezed out of the current board agenda. This committee works closely with the company's chief strategy/business development officer, CTO, and CMO to monitor management's framework for evaluating new business models and how technology may help accelerate them. "Board and committee members cannot be expected to have all the answers," says Steve Miller. "But they need to ask the right questions of management."

In the end, referring to a board "technology committee," or even focusing on tech as an end in itself, misses the mark. Technology is only one tool in an overall new capability we should demand of boards. While boards must now offer savvy and skills in new technology, this is only of value if used to stimulate innovation, to see what's coming for business, and to encourage management to prepare for the future.

Adapted from *Corporate Board Member* Third Quarter 2015, Volume 18, Number 3.

Boards Need Help Adapting to Disruptive Marketplaces

Technology has created the age of the marketplace, which enables the maker of the product or service to connect with the consumer directly. If boards are not part of their companies' innovation efforts, the marketplace model threatens to disrupt many businesses. These marketplaces extend to nearly all industries: Uber and Lyft created a new marketplace for taxis; Airbnb and Home Away in hospitality; eBay for various items; and Etsy for crafts. Even the sourcing of board members and advisors is being handled in a marketplace by ExecRank, which poses a threat to search firms.

The marketplace model is not merely a new iteration of technology, but a fundamental recasting of commerce. If management is still focused on competitors from a year or even six months ago, a marketplace challenger may not even show up on the radar. In order to adopt and embrace this shift, companies will either need to partner with a marketplace company or decide to disintermediate themselves.

To achieve this change, boards could create a new technology and innovation committee. This committee would look not just at technology trends, but also at encouraging management to think about what may be around the corner. A technology discussion is a natural fit with a board's strategic oversight duties and can bring in fresh thinking from the very top. The tech committee's charter would assign it to look at innovative trends and business models—such as e-commerce and marketplaces—competitive dynamics and how technology can be exploited for the future.

Boards would seek directors with a breadth of experience for this committee, not just tech experts. The ideal candidate would be a proven executive with solid exposure to cyber, social media and mobile, big-data analytics and e-commerce. Boards may also consider looking at technology industry leaders, CMOs, CIOs, CSOs and consultants who specialize in tech. Mixing deep technology expertise with a former or current CMO or a business development expert on the committee may cover these bases. Boards may look outside traditional director circles for skills.

This new committee should meet around four times a year and have three or four members with the above backgrounds. But the committee should be different from the others in some crucial ways. While most information that boards receive is inward facing—such as company reports, financials and filings—the tech committee should have an outward focus. Members should review industry and analyst reports on the company and its sector. The committee would focus on maximizing a company's margins and potential growth areas. The committee would also discuss technology risk issues, such as cyber crime and hacking, but also address risks that the company business model could overlook.

A new technology committee needs to remain consistent with the board's role of performing oversight and not actually create strategy or become an operating management function. Instead, the committee should challenge management's thinking to ensure the company has addressed the risks of rapid change.

A technology committee meets a vital need in the modern boardroom. It brings focused knowledge of technology to address the strategy and innovation oversight that is too often knocked off the current board agenda. This committee should work closely with the company's chief strategy or business development officer, CTO and CMO to monitor management's framework for evaluating new business models and how technology may help accelerate them. It should also look at adding a marketplace component to the company's current business plan to stay relevant for the long term, if the company does not have one already.
The marketplace model poses many risks to companies that do not adapt quickly. But a committee focused on technology and innovation can help boards find new opportunities and prosper.

Adapted from *Agenda*, November 16, 2015.

Betsy Atkins

The Cost of Information Misgovernance and What You Can Do about It

Information governance—historically a bottom-up practice and now the responsibility of Governance, Risk and Compliance (GRC) managers—has been pushing its way into boardrooms around the world. Sarbanes-Oxley, HIPAA, The Basel II accords, and similar regulations have triggered this trend.

The problem is that the concerned parties rarely speak the same technical language. Modern enterprise information management systems are helping to address the problem but there are still a few secrets to success. Here are some things to keep in mind during your initiatives.

The terms "corporate governance" and "information governance" no doubt sound similar. Many people focus only on the "governance" aspect of both, and assume that they are different names for the same discipline. But for too long those who specialize in both fields have paid too little attention to each other—a disinterest that courts and regulators are now forcing to an end. Corporate governance—the role of boards and top management in overseeing, administering, and monitoring a company, is very much of a "top-down" field. Information governance, which oversees the performance and risk management of information technology (IT) systems, would seem to be a very "bottom-up," tactical item at the bottom of a board's agenda. Yet IT and data management have been pushing their way up on that boardroom agenda for some time.

How Technology Became the Board's Business
The first IT moves we saw in the boardroom came a decade ago, when the technology costs and potential dangers of Y2K problems became a boardroom concern. But the costs and legal liability for managing (or mismanaging) electronic data did not fade with the millennium, and have in fact spiked higher over the past several years.

The federal Sarbanes-Oxley Act of 2002, particularly its Section 404, mandated a strong internal control environment, including the electronic data needed to prove it. The Health Insurance Portability and Accountability Act (HIPAA), which became effective in 2003, imposed tough data privacy and protection mechanisms for any businesses related to health care. The Basel II accords on banking in 2004 required robust

106

data storage and retrieval capability. The Personal Data Privacy and Security Act, and its subsequent updates, set complex information security rules for government agencies and their private contractors.

Legal requirements on how companies must preserve and produce data also grew rapidly. In late 2006, new amendments to the Federal Rules of Civil Procedure (FRCP) regarding electronic discovery of evidence became effective. These codified, and in some ways simplified, electronic evidence discovery matters. But the new FRCP rules also forced companies to better organize their data management processes.

The High Cost of Information "Misgovernance"

Corporations have learned the hard way that these requirements have teeth. In 2008, non-compliance with FRCP data discovery demands in litigation cost UBS Warburg $29 million, and Merck a whopping $253 million. But even playing by the new data governance rules can cost a company if the information is badly retained and organized. Recently, a Fortune 100 corporation, in seeking to acquire a competitor, learned a hard lesson on information governance when it scrambled to meet government antitrust disclosure demands. Over 150 workers spent 10 weeks reviewing material, including 1.5 million emails alone.

Organizations not directly involved in an investigation also suffer nowadays if they lack modern information governance processes. A small government agency had only peripheral involvement in the investigation of Freddie Mac. The general counsel of this small, under-funded office had signed off on an e-discovery request to search their email and files, assuming the cost would be minor. But the inaccessibility of the data required an army of attorneys and staff to perform a hands-on physical review—all billed by the hour. The "minor" cost came to $6 million, and this for a non-party to the litigation. By the way, this agency sought relief for this crippling cost, but was turned down by an appeals court. The court's reasoning? The general counsel should have known what he was letting the agency in for when he approved an open-ended e-discovery process.

"Should have known" is an apt description of the evolving philosophy driving information governance and corporate governance into the same room. Regulators have established that well-organized, well-preserved, accessible electronic data is now expected as fundamental to any well-governed company. Courts and plaintiff attorneys have followed this lead. They now routinely demand thorough, timely review and disclosure of discoverable electronic evidence. The question today for corporate boards is whether their company's e-discovery infrastructure is able to deliver.

IT and Corporate Governance
Similar Concerns, But Different Languages

Among the greatest problems facing the board on information governance (and especially e-discovery issues) are the differing perspectives of the company departments involved. The IT staff is often directed toward its specific priorities. Reliability, practicality, cost efficiency, and the ability of new software to interact with legacy technology are among these touchstones of good information governance.

The IT staff, of necessity, has its own technical language to explain these processes, components, and priorities. For years, board meetings have seen "Dilbert" cartoon moments of tech staff briefing directors in their own, specialized techie language, while the board members' eyes slowly glaze over. One data management vendor (who will remain nameless) boasts that its "scale-out grid architecture" offers "a single-instance indexed repository and supports delta versioning." With a sales pitch like this, it's no wonder that board members just approve IT budgets and hope for the best.

But this "best" may not be the best for good governance oversight of data, or the current demands of e-discovery. Corporate governance has data oversight priorities that often parallel those of IT, but differ in some key aspects. The board role here is shaped by the needs of company compliance and legal staff. The latter are aware that the vast amount of data generated by a modern corporation serves an ongoing purpose. It can prove that oversight and corporate compliance have been properly handled in vital areas, such as regulatory rules, accounting, tax law, M&A, risk management, and the board itself.

But company counsel and governance, risk, and compliance (GRC) staff have further specific IT demands. First are smart, best-practice data retention policies. IT measures itself in part by how safely it can store away all those emails, documents, memos, and so on. More data to be stored means adding more storage capability. Yet this is not only costly, but adds needless legal risk. Even with the best information management system, the more material you cache the more you have to inventory, evaluate—and possibly mismanage. An e-discovery demand that prompts a general "data dump" could include sensitive, compromising material that legally need not have been retained—but as long as it's in the servers, you have to produce it.

Why We Call it a "Data Retention," Policy, Not "Data Deletion"

Good corporate governance of IT, then, demands a comprehensive, uniform, legally savvy retention policy that deletes as much nonessential material as quickly as possible. But notice that we call it a data "retention" policy—not data "deletion." A wise corporate governance approach focuses on the data you need to keep as much as that you should toss. Work with counsel to establish protocols on where and how different types of data will be stored (and how it should not be stored); classification and segregation of data based on legal retention schedules, sensitivity, and operational needs; and proper procedures for deletion. Also, a "legal hold" policy must be able to kick in immediately should a court or regulatory action be launched (too often a memo from counsel saying "Don't delete x data" brings replies like "what x data?" or "too late.").

Shaping Board-Friendly Information Governance

Conventional data management and information governance, thus, don't fit well with the board's corporate oversight role. Manually wrestling with things like database management, classification protocols, purging schedules, and tracking various email and text message platforms is no task for the lay business folks in the boardroom. The immersion in time and tech demanded just isn't practical.

This mismatch grows even worse when dealing with the e-discovery requirements of litigation. Directors will want to know if legal holds on data are effectively in place, and whether material not covered under the hold, or legally privileged, is properly segregated. They'll want to know how much time and cost will be involved in the e-discovery review (and probably respond with groans). And the board will want to know why it's spent so much money on fancy data management tech, only to have e-discovery require hours of manual, costly, erratic data chasing.

Traditional IT systems do a good job of warehousing data, but are poor at easily finding and retrieving data to meet the demands of e-discovery. I've found that there is a way to combine the needs of information governance and corporate governance for the benefit of both—modern electronic information management systems. These new tools not only streamline, cut costs, and improve results, but also give the board the "dashboard" tools it needs for effective IT oversight. One of the biggest governance demands in recent years has been for simple, but revealing indicators that allow busy board members to gain a good read on complex functions. Audit, finance, risk management, and internal controls are some of the intimidating, technical fields being boiled down to a usable "dashboard" of measures the board can use for oversight. Now, it's the turn of information governance.

Requirements for a Modern e-Discovery Platform

New "intelligent" information management platforms, such as StoredIQ, PSS Systems, and Symantec Enterprise Vault are meeting these governance objectives. These products must meet several vital goals:

- Comply with all corporate policy and government regulations. Those who interface with the system must be able to know exactly what information is stored, and where.
- Reduce risk, preempt litigation and avoid fines. These are based on the ability of the technology to identify and secure documents as required by law or possible litigation.
- Help ensure that valuable business information is safe and accessible to authorized personnel only, meeting regulatory compliance requirements and corporate access policies.
- Segregate older, infrequently accessed material to less expensive storage facilities.
- Automatically enforce record retention schedules through automated identification and retention of records to permanent storage.
- "Clean house" by actively identifying and destroying documents whose age exceeds document retention policies.

According to Laura Lukaczyk, venture investor in StoredIQ, "The need for non-manual discovery is clear. Just about every company faces investigation and the shear growth of information pushes the tipping point for transitioning to an automated data collection process. In addition, forward leaning information technology groups are already deploying storage in the cloud where a solution to digitally manage information in discovery is key. The StoredIQ solution is fast to deploy and delivers a fast ROI according to our company case studies."

These next generation products meet these demands in another way—by offering effective interface between those in the company involved in information governance and e-discovery. As noted, IT staff, corporate counsel, risk, and compliance staff traditionally kept to their own silos, with the board often not even in the same farmyard. The intelligent data management platforms of today are designed to meet the needs of all these parties, and to be uniformly accessible to them. For example, litigation staff may want to run "pre-e-discovery" on a potential litigation, checking to see what data is hidden away before opposing counsel actually makes its demands. A solution like StoredIQ makes this possible. It can run early, query-based analyses of discoverable material from a broad database, quickly, easily, and thoroughly. This is a powerful litigation tool for the firm, saving time and cost, and helping counsel, management, and the board better gauge the company's exposure.

Boards of directors will likely never have the time and skills required to become technical information governance experts. But with the new world of intelligent data management, and the tools it offers, directors shouldn't need to.

Adapted from *CMS Wire* June 25, 2009.

Information security is a big issue and boards will soon become liable to prove they have best practice security measures and compliance programs in place. The risks and costs are huge, from brand and reputational customer records to potential loss of key intellectual property that can be pirated via confidential cyber theft.

The Fear Factor of Corporate Responsibility

Over the past year, information security has become one of corporate America's most serious challenges. The increasingly interconnected nature of conducting electronic business, including a massive rise in telecommunications, makes it harder to track who is doing what on company systems and networks. Layoffs may create disgruntled workers who may still have access to vital electronic information. In fact, attacks from both malicious hackers and insiders gone bad are on the rise.

To date, the immediate revenue impact of security lapses, mostly from downtime of critical systems, has been well documented. According to the 2002 FBI/Computer Security Institute's Computer Crime and Security Survey, U.S. companies and government agencies reported an annual loss of $170.8 million due to theft of proprietary information—more than any other type of attack on their computer systems. PricewaterhouseCoopers reported that hacker attacks alone cost the world economy a staggering $1.6 trillion in 2001.

But corporate America hasn't even begun to feel the effects of a new aftershock: legal liability. Businesses will have to prove they have "best practice" security measures in place in order to avoid paying out millions in damages. There are board governance and legal aspects of security breaches. I will suggest steps organizations can take to reduce legal liability. More than ever, boards (audit committees) are required to perform stringent due diligence and are accountable for the security measures they have in place.

Mistakes and Mischief Increase Liability

One of an organization's most valuable and perhaps most dangerous assets are its employees. They have power. They can create, access and deploy extremely valuable information to customers, partners, one another. Using this power, they can also jeopardize security, expose company files intentionally or otherwise and thus open the company to lawsuits. With power should come accountability; there's the rub. In addition to companies filing insurance claims seeking reimbursement for losses for data leaks and data theft, we're now seeing lawsuits within and between organizations due to accusations of hacking. This has opened the litigation floodgates. As a result, companies need to manage end users to ensure everyone's protection.

Every day we're seeing news stories about a major loss of confidential information from well-known organizations such as Cisco, Genentech, Hewlett-Packard, and Merrill Lynch. These breaches of confidence are not only extremely embarrassing but also jeopardize the very existence of the organization. Inadequate security procedures can lead to the public disclosure of proprietary information, financial loss to business partners and customers, the spread of harmful computer viruses, and distributed denial-of-service attacks. The 2002 FBI/Computer Security Institute survey results indicate that merely installing security products does not guarantee protection from attacks. Although 89 percent of respondents use firewalls and 60 percent use intrusion detection systems, 40 percent reported attacks coming from outside the organization. Then, there are the honest mistakes. Take for example:

- Cisco released its financial results in February due to the click of the mouse. An internal memo related to the quarterly earnings was inadvertently sent to more Cisco employees than intended, and company officials became concerned that so many people had seen the information that they could be in violation of Securities and Exchange Commission guidelines, according to a Cisco spokeswoman
- Genentech didn't have such a happy ending in April as its shares got hammered after research abstracts prepared for the upcoming annual meeting of the American Society of Clinical Oncology were leaked. This may or may not have been intentional, but it wasn't due to a hacker or a virus
- And what about Hewlett-Packard CEO Carly Fiorina's memo to her employees in March about company status that made it into many, many more inboxes than those of her employees—such as those of the press? That employee was identified and immediately fired
- New York Attorney General Eliot Spitzer dropped a bombshell on Merrill Lynch in April when he publicly displayed a series of

email messages that had been sent among Merrill Lynch research staffers. Spitzer used them as proof that analysts were recommending stocks they didn't believe in

These events have forced a wave of internal legal personnel and external regulators to turn up the pressure on due diligence. Organizations take risks on their intellectual assets, so it's crucial for them to know where information is going, to whom and why. Ironically, as senior executives become more accountable regarding their corporate digital assets, they will likely turn to their technologists to solve the problems.

The Buck Stops with the Employer
Are corporations vicariously liable for the conduct of their employees? Under many circumstances, the answer is "yes." Employee misconduct may leave companies facing liability for sexual harassment, defamation, violations of intellectual property rights (including misappropriation of trade secrets), hacking, and even violations of the securities laws.

While financial gain may be the most common motive for abusing confidential information, other reasons for leaking information include the desire to run up a deal's price, scuttle a deal or even gain prestige. Take, for example, the situation in April in which Vivendi Universal agreed to sell its Italian pay-TV operations to Rupert Murdoch's News Corp. The deal would benefit the companies in more ways than one. If completed, it would end litigation between the two firms, including a $1.1 billion lawsuit that saw a Murdoch firm accused of corporate-sponsored computer hacking.

If anything should be made clear to corporate executives by the events over the past months, it is that the concept of putting up a wall isn't enough. Gaining an understanding about intellectual property, where it resides and how it is moving throughout the network gives the company some chance of protecting it.

Regulatory Activity Helping to Drive the Legal Boundaries
Regulations implementing the privacy and security provisions of the Gramm-Leach-Bliley Act of 1999 and the proposed security regulations implementing the Health Insurance Portability and Accountability Act of 1996 (HIPAA) put a framework and some elbow grease around legal issues. The GLB regulations require board and management involvement

in the development and implementation of an information security program. For example, the board must, among other things, approve a financial institution's written information security program and oversee the development, implementation and maintenance of a financial institution's information security program.

The Health Insurance Portability and Accountability Act mandated regulations governing privacy, security and electronic transactions standards for health care information. HIPAA touches virtually all health care organizations, requiring them to reassess their computer systems and internal procedures for compliance. Breaches of medical privacy such as press disclosures of individuals' records, network hacking incidents, patient consent issues, and misdirected patient emails fueled this concern.

What we're seeing is a way for a regulatory authority to force organizations to take security seriously by mandating that companies protect their intellectual assets from threats, hazards and unauthorized access.

Boards Set Policies, Management Enforces Them
After carefully assessing potential enterprise liability, including potential liability for sexual harassment, copyright infringement, and defamation arising out of the misconduct of employees, companies should consider ways to reduce their legal exposure. The key for management is to develop, implement and enforce an e-mail/Internet use policy, making sure that the employer acts promptly when it learns of employee misconduct. Organizations should have defined policies on incident response. The monitoring of user behavior is legal and does not violate employees' constitutional rights.

One approach to enforcement of an email/Internet use policy is to engage in monitoring of employee email/Internet usage. Generally speaking, in the United States an employer's legitimate business justification for monitoring (*e.g.*, guarding against improper use of a company's email system, or keeping tabs on employee productivity) will be sufficient to override an employee's privacy expectations so long as the employer properly implements its monitoring program. Proper implementation may require companies to take policy measures and set appropriate expectations to try to prevent information leakage, such as the following:

- Include in the company's acceptable policy notice to employees that the company owns the computer system, that all emails, computer files, etc., are the property of the employer, that systems are primarily for business purposes, and that the company reserves the right to review and disclose matters sent over the system and stored on the system
- Specify in the acceptable use policy that the computer system must not be used for distribution of certain content (*e.g.*, acceptable use policies often prohibit defamatory e-mail, distribution of copyrighted material, etc.)
- Be careful not to limit the basis on which the company is permitted to monitor employees' computer use. Doing so enables workers to argue that the scope of employee consent to monitoring was restricted by company policy
- Require employees to sign a form stating that they have read and understand the corporate email policy and agree to its terms as a condition of access to, and use of, the computer system. The form should state that a breach of confidentiality is not only a violation of company policy, but also a violation of the law if a person acts on his or her own behalf, and uses that information for financial gain and/or shares that information with others who then might act on the information

A court is highly unlikely to conclude that an employee has a reasonable expectation of privacy in his email communications when the employer has a policy clearly stating that such communications are subject to monitoring. As such, employers are free to monitor their employees' use of their networks so long as the company does not violate labor and anti-discrimination laws, for example, by targeting union organizers or minorities.

Conclusion: Monitoring User Behavior and Assets Doesn't Violate Any Constitutional Rights

Gaining an understanding about your intellectual property, where it resides, and how it is moving throughout the network gives you some chance of protecting it. Measured use of monitoring technology can contribute to a company's efforts to identify objectionable employee conduct before it rises to an actionable level. On the other hand, companies should be aware that pervasive monitoring could lead to employees being overly sensitive and perhaps critical about the scrutiny. Toward this end, companies should consider various strategies to protect themselves. Simply reserving the *right* to monitor email in the future while *actually* monitoring only in limited circumstances such as when monitoring is necessary to investigate reports of misuse; other steps might include establishing documentation requirements to ensure management awareness of employee behavior that may pose a risk to the company. With emerging technology evolving rapidly, only high-end analytical tools will enable organizations to keep up with the massive amounts of data they will need to analyze.

Adapted from *Directors Monthly* September 2002.

Directors need to know the cyber risks from both inside and outside the company. They need to be briefed by management, discuss and agree on the amount of risk they feel the company should take, and then create a policy that adheres to that risk and protects the shareholders.

Board Focus on Cyber Security

The Game Has Changed
In this new Internet age, business never stops. With the emergence of virtual, mobile and cloud technologies, the traditional perimeter of business has disappeared. The addition of these new technologies has forever changed how we live and work. As business leaders, we need to embrace these new technologies to improve productivity and, ultimately, share price. However, the manner in which these new technologies are utilized needs board-level attention, to set and measure the thresholds of risk. Business leaders tend to underestimate risk if they haven't been impacted by it. There is a stubborn insistence on touching the hot stove before believing it hurts. Risks are increasing in a global environment that operates 24/7.

Threats to organizations' assets come from a variety of sources and need to be addressed at the board level with a program that has support and funding.

Risk Evaluation
What are the risks and where do they come from? There is a tendency, fueled by the media, to focus on technical exploits that are out "in the wild", as if the only risk of concern is from a zero-day exploit. The reality is much more mundane, and also much more complex. While it is certainly important to ensure that technical risks from outside the organization are mitigated, it is equally important to manage risk posed by insiders and third party relationships. It doesn't matter if your assets were compromised by a sexy new exploit or by an employee losing a laptop with client data: the data is still compromised.

Know Your Cyber Risks
An organization's greatest threat is in not knowing their risks. Business functions that were traditionally performed on paper are migrating online, which requires a different approach in asset protection. A locked door may have protected sensitive paper files, but is of little use in

118

protecting data that is stored online. Organizations, under pressure to provide online services, may fail to perform an informed risk assessment that factors in technology concerns. The ability to quickly access a vast amount of data from any location also means that there is a greater risk for unauthorized access. The advantages become the disadvantages. Although business risks vary among different organizations, some basic risk elements are:

- Theft of intellectual property
- Fraud
- Sabotage

Know Where Your Risks Originate - External Threats

To accommodate an increasingly mobile workforce, organizations provide many services online, which make it convenient for personnel to perform their work. This also makes it easier for undetected, unauthorized access. In the virtual world, there is no security guard at the door checking credentials before permitting access.

Media attention focuses on the threat from malicious hackers who target any system that is vulnerable to the latest exploit. The real threat is more serious: motivated attackers who are specifically targeting your organization and have the time/skill to succeed and evade detection. This Advanced Persistent Threat (APT) is a serious risk that must be addressed. The motivation for bored hackers may be to see if their exploits succeed, but the motivation behind APT attackers is to gain access to your data for long periods of time. APT attackers won't care how they gained access, just that they did. They also won't be interested in bragging rights, so you may never know that your data was compromised!

Insider Threats

It's easier to recognize threats from external sources since outsiders are not usually authorized to access internal information. It is much more difficult to gauge threats from internal people and to recognize characteristics of insiders who may compromise data, either through ignorance or deliberately

Risk Scenarios

Scenario 1: A new hire emails confidential client information to a personal email account, to work on from home. When discovered; the new hire claimed to have not known it was against company policy and had not been required to have information security training. What are the risks and potential business impact for not ensuring that every new hire receives information security training?

- Breach of contract—financial liability
- Privacy breach—legal liability

Scenario 2: A business unit decides to bring in a new contractor to assist during a busy season. Because of time constraints, they do not wait for the background check before allowing the contractor to start, and provide access to system resources. What are the risks and potential business impact by not following the new-hire process to completion?

- Could allow a criminal access to the organization's systems
- Breach of contract—Financial liability

Scenario 3: An associate takes his laptop on vacation. He lets his family use the computer to read email. One of his children uses it to go to a number of gaming sites and message boards. What are the risks and potential business impact of not restricting the use of a business computer to business purposes only?

- Malware could be loaded on the associate's laptop, infecting other machines when reconnected to the network
- Confidential data could be stolen from the associate's laptop
- Associate's user credentials could be stolen and used to breach the system at a later date

Scenario 4: An associate has installed a webcam and Skype on his computer for videoconferencing. What are the risks and potential business impact to allowing associates to install videoconferencing technology?

- Potential for webcam to be accessed remotely to spy on the associate

- Compliance violation (lack of business record, cannot audit Skype use)
- Skype is not compliant with standards
- Risk of peer-to-peer software spreading malware

Risk Tolerance Must Be Defined at the Top

A clear articulation of the organization's broad risk tolerance must be reviewed at the board level. Boards mitigate risks through reviewing appropriate internal policies that the organization will meet or exceed.

On the network and Internet front, risks and network vulnerabilities are constantly shifting. An effective information security program needs to adapt to these changes. Most organizations' biggest challenges are to discover what is on their network. Vulnerabilities are found at too slow a rate to manage or react to them and often solutions are not immediately apparent.

The good news is that many new automated network security-monitoring technologies, such as Tenable's SecurityCenter Continuous View, can meet these challenges. These technologies can automate the audit, measurement, and reporting on security and compliance goals. It is important to look for technologies that can gather information/data in multiple ways, be "always on" or continuous, and are easily adaptable to emerging technologies.

Board and audit committees are well versed on SOX 404 financial controls. In this millennium they must also be trained on a framework, such as ISO 27000, to evaluate if the cyber security of the shareholders' assets is complete and robust.

Conclusion

A proactive vulnerability management program that addresses specific business needs of the organization will go far to provide real value to the organization. Planning requires effort, but poor planning results in wasted resources.

First published in this volume.

CHAPTER 6: EFFECTIVE LEGAL OVERSIGHT

The board should consider when to use outside legal counsel when the in-house general counsel may be conflicted by loyalty to management. The directors need to proactively assess and understand the "legal environment" inside the company regarding true compliance. Are the policies on business ethics and code of conduct embraced, understood, and enforced?

Warding Off Shareholder Suits

How does the board avoid shareholder lawsuits? By having committed, engaged, and knowledgeable directors who bring unique perspective and experience to the table, directors who invest time to educate themselves on the company's products and market dynamics, who can do informed listening and contribute business judgment to help grow the company. The shareholders expect directors to contribute their board governance experience and counsel on such sophisticated matters as acquisitions, integrations, complex financing, etc. Experience in fighting shareholder lawsuits helps, too, as it enables board members to anticipate actions to avoid, problems and pitfalls. The sharp increase in the number of shareholder lawsuits is indicative of aggressive plaintiffs rather than endemic problems in corporate America. Today two percent of our GNP is spent on lawsuits!

To protect companies and shareholders more aggressively from this litigious overload, which at best is distracting and at worst is financially costly, I suggest that boards make better use of outside counsel.

Let's focus on board governance and how the board interacts with—and what it can expect from—in-house counsel and external counsel. These expectations are not always clear. The role of the director of a public company is clear: We are fiduciaries for the shareholders. Our objective is to oversee and contribute business judgment to maximize the company's return on investment and long-term growth. The role of the outside director is well defined. Equally, the role of the board audit committee is now crisply defined. The Sarbanes-Oxley Act makes it very clear that the audit committee hires and reviews the outside audit firm. It serves as an independent check and balance on the corporation's finances, dedicated to serving the best interest of the shareholders.

The question arises, where is the analogous check and balance function in the corporate and boardroom structure for the legal advisory function? Is the corporation's inside counsel serving the board of directors or the corporation first? Who is inside counsel's client? I maintain that the corporation is the inside counsel's client. After all, the corporation hires, fires, and is the organizational structure in which inside counsel operates and reports. The corporation sets inside counsel's priorities, whether it's negotiating distribution channel contracts or preparing patent applications.

Inside counsel frequently has the task of damage control, to solve all the ugly problems and protect the company on issues before they require board action. Inside counsel also creates an environment for fostering the legal well being of the firm—ranging from compliance with regulations and the law to setting the principles of the company's business ethics and code of conduct. Creating the appropriate environment of legal control is essential for the long-term success of the enterprise and contributes to an atmosphere that will protect against vulnerability to shareholder lawsuits and other lawsuits that arise in the normal conduct of business.

The conflicts arise only when there is a question of poor corporate conduct or judgment by management that surface to the board. Then the question the board asks is where was our inside counsel? Why wasn't he or she aware of such abuses as:

- Our sales force purloining the competitor's price list
- Our sales force engaged in illegal foreign corrupt practices

- Management's recommendation to have the company's pension fund invest in the company's new convertible debt offering

Whose job is it to advise the board when the company may be straying into the gray zone? If directors rely only on inside counsel, are they doing a thorough job in discharging their duty of care? Isn't relying only on inside counsel akin to the audit committee relying solely on the CFO and not checking with the outside auditors?

I believe that inside counsel, when discharging the responsibility of putting the most persuasive argument forward for the corporation, cannot be completely objective. The independent check and balance function of the board may best be served by outside counsel. I suggest that outside counsel should be an available independent guidepost or resource to inform the board of conflicts, legal risks and improper practices.

I propose that the board governance committee should have powers similar to those granted to the audit committee. They should be authorized to retain their own independent outside counsel, distinguished from outside counsel retained by the company, if in special cases they feel they have need for additional advice.

The governance committee is charged with safeguarding the soul of the corporation. Does the company have the proper code of business ethics and code of conduct? Has the company provided compliance training so its employees understand the corporation's business mores? For example, are policies in place against sexual harassment? Is a whistle-blower process published? Are policies on theft of intellectual property and competitive information understood? What about explaining what foreign corrupt practices means in practical terms? Does the company have an information security and document retention policy, and is it understood? Is it enforced?

The governance committee is responsible for overseeing how the corporation is governed for the shareholders. An independent legal resource needs to be identified and authorization for the board to utilize it needs to be established. I liken such authorization to the checks and balances built into our government structure.

Ultimately, the board must make the business judgments and decisions it thinks best serve the interests of the shareholders to build a sound and robust business. Directors must discharge their duty of care and duty of loyalty responsibly and to do this, they need clear access to objective legal advice for the oversight of the company's legal decisions. Oddly, even in today's governance-charged business climate, this remains a gray area in the boardroom that no one seems to be discussing. Lack of legal resources for the board is the trap door in the Trojan horse that inadvertently leaves the corporation vulnerable to bad management decisions.

Directors cannot abdicate to their legal advisors their responsibility to make business judgments, but without clearly identified independent legal advisors, things can go astray. I recommend that an empowered governance committee whose function encompasses legal issues would enhance the board's preparedness for avoiding shareholder lawsuits.

In this new era of corporate governance, whistleblowers are given special protective status under corporate codes of business conduct and ethics. In distinguishing between meritorious and fictionalized claims of wrongdoing, directors cannot allow for a decision void. We need to clarify explicitly the roles of inside counsel and external counsel as they relate to the board. I recommend that just as the Sarbanes-Oxley legislation has clarified and strengthened the audit committee responsibility to hire external auditors, so too should the governance committee be responsible for the company's code of conduct and have regular and direct access to external counsel.

Adapted from *Directorship* February 2003.

Is It Time For a Board "Cyber-Security" Committee?

In December, Sony Pictures revealed that it has been the victim of a massive cyber attack, with sophisticated hackers raiding the company networks for coming movies, corporate financial and salary records, and personal information about major stars (Sylvester Stallone even found his Social Security number leaked worldwide).

In an article for the BBC's business blog, British corporate consulting expert Lucy Marcus went to the heart of the governance implications. "At every board meeting this month someone is bound to ask, either during the meeting or in a quiet aside, 'Could we be the next Sony?'" The saddest aspect of this is that corporate boards of companies around the world have *already* been asking much the same question for the past several years, only changing the name of the victim.

Just the past 12 months have seen one massive corporate security breach after another. Major retailers (Target, Home Depot), e-commerce sites (eBay), and financial institutions (JP Morgan) have all been victims. While the trend of breach after breach is unsettling, the far more important fact is that all of these attacks share the same multi-step blueprint for the attack.

In each case, the attack began by compromising one person with credentialed access—typically a partner or an employee. Then, that access was used to create an infected node that could burrow deeper into the network. This would then steal data stored internally, or infect additional systems that capture the target data, such as point-of-sale terminals. While it is still too early to tell how the massive Sony Pictures hack was organized, it likely used the same essential outline.

Taken individually, digital security breaches serve as a warning for executives and security professionals to remain vigilant. However, when every major breach shares the same telltale strategy, it is a sign that there is something more fundamentally broken in enterprise security that must be addressed.

Here is some of the damage that management and corporate governance oversight systems were unable to prevent:

eBay.

> 145 million records compromised.
>
> Multiple employee login credentials were accessed, and used to dig deeper into the network, and ultimately steal customer data.

JP Morgan.

> 76 million records compromised.
>
> Access was gained through an employee laptop, and then spread across the network to find customer contact information.

Target.

> 70 million records accessed.
>
> Network was initially compromised via a partner (using their HVAC vendor's credentials). This then spread through the network, and pushed malware to the Target point-of-sale systems.

Home Depot.

> 56 million records compromised.
>
> Network was breached via a partner's credentials, and malware delivered to point-of-sale systems. The malware was a variant of the malware used at Target.

Michaels stores.

> Three million records compromised.
>
> Michaels has not confirmed the details of how they were breached, only that there was a network breach, and affected terminals were all compromised with previously unknown malware.

Neiman Marcus.

> One million records compromised.
>
> Network hacked and malware pushed down to the point-of-sale systems.

There are several important similarities in these attacks, all suggesting that your company data security protections need stronger oversight.

Security looks for the first step, but misses the lifecycle of an attack.
Traditional online security structures attempt to detect and block
malicious payloads (either a piece of malware or vulnerability exploit).
In the past, this was a very sensible approach, because the initial payload
and the attack were one in the same. A basic programming query was
fired at a vulnerable website, and the attacker gained a list of usernames
and passwords. Malware was installed on a victim, and the hackers
quickly spammed her contact list, and that was the end of the episode.

In a modern attack, the initial compromise is just a means to a much
larger end. The first compromise provides the beachhead for the larger
attack, which will be driven by a criminal who has done his homework
on your organization. This can then play out over weeks, months, even
years. The vast majority of security technologies are not designed to see
the so-called "long con" of an attack. Even though the security industry
continues to develop more and more advanced methods of detecting
individual pieces of malware, there is still too little ability to see the larger
attack that follows *after* the malware. The attackers are playing chess,
while your information security protections are still playing checkers.

There are infinite opportunities for security systems to fail.

As computing and business has evolved, the "attackable" areas of the
enterprise have become nearly impossible to secure. Employees use
mobile devices that are routinely outside the corporate firewalls.
Corporate applications and data are increasingly both inside and outside
the perimeter. Partners and customers need access to corporate
applications and data in order to be competitive and efficient. Also, of
course, attackers are constantly cooking up new attacks and strategies to
evade detection.

All of this adds up to a near infinite number of chances for attackers to get
the initial exploit of an attack past security. This then enables the internal
phase of the targeted attack, beyond the protection of outward-facing
firewalls, IPSs, and malware sandboxes. Those who design prisons
dedicate at most a few weeks or months to making them escape-proof.
Those jailed in them, however, may have a life sentence of time to devise
workarounds.

Smart hackers will use your own security protocols against you.

While security products can generate tons of data, it is often difficult to see the forest for the trees. For example, Target had indications that a new piece of malware was found in their network, but the context of the larger attack remained unclear. The Neiman Marcus breach generated thousands of low-priority informational alerts that were seen as false positives by the security team because the suspicious files looked like approved files that were allowed to be on the system. In these cases and many others, it is obvious that data is not the same as insight. Security teams are often placed in the untenable position of trying to piece together conclusions from large amounts of data. Such a large amount of data is sometimes beyond the scope of what security was designed to detect.

Here is a hard truth I have learned about corporate boards—directors really do not understand company security issues. In fact, most top corporate managers do not either. They fail to see all the resources that they must protect, what needs protecting, and just how vulnerable they actually are. This gap is even greater when it comes to the digital assets of the modern corporation.

There is no denying that it is difficult for directors to provide the oversight needed in this digital era. Online security has become incredibly complicated, and corporate directors may not even know the fundamental distinctions between the various types and motivations of online intrusions. For example, a basic hack may just be trying to steal credit card info, the digital equivalent of a "smash and grab" thief.

A higher-level, sophisticated cyber thief, on the other hand, may be targeting a particularly high-value corporate asset. This could be a seismic analysis of your oil/gas field, or a compound your pharmaceutical company has been working on for years. There may be cyber intrusions with national security or political aims, an attempt by foreign powers to access defense information or technology in your system, or an international hack to embarrass your company (as may have been the case with Sony America). Your board likely lacks the expertise and oversight system to know the difference between a casual and a deep cyberthreat, or know when data lost is something valuable— versus a breach that could completely put you out of business.

Step one for every board is to understand is that it is supposed to be offering oversight on these risks as part of its fiduciary duty. Your audit committee knows that it needs internal controls, like those mandated by Sarbanes-Oxley Section 404, to protect corporate assets. Likewise, the board now needs to assure internal controls to protect the corporation's cyber assets.

The stakes are high. In today's financial control environment, the chance of someone embezzling a large sum from the company through financial wrongdoing is fairly small. Yes, it happens, but it has grown far more difficult to successfully pull off such a scam. However, the amount of assets stolen and compromised through cyber-breaches is astronomical in comparison. A study found that up to $21 trillion in global assets could be at risk from cybercrime. What is needed is a solid board structure for monitoring and managing cyber risk in the company. Oversight of cyber-risk at the board level is part of a larger mandate boards have faced over the past decade, that of properly managing risk overall. The economic crisis of 2008-2009 found many boards caught unaware of the financial and market risks their companies were exposed to, and board oversight structures have spent the past few years rushing to catch up.

Audit committees were seen as the most natural slot for the risk oversight portfolio. The committee performs a wide range of oversight responsibilities, from financial controls and compliance to other corporate risks. However, I believe there is a big gap in most audit committees when it comes to understanding the unique cyber-security vulnerability of companies. Audit, by definition, deals in financial figures, and issues that do not lend themselves to a spreadsheet can be difficult for them to oversee.

If your board chooses to make its audit committee the home of cyber-security oversight, start by upgrading its capabilities. Audit committees need to better understand how security threats strike so they can provide better oversight and risk management. The first step I recommend is a series of committee briefings so "cyber security" is demystified and better understood. The company's objectives to protect critical information, client identities, and financial vulnerability should be discussed. I also recommend requesting a security plan that can be audited.

However, given the complexity and dangers involved, I think the time has come for boards to create a dedicated cyber/security technology committee. Boards currently have three standard standing committees (audit, compensation, governance/nominating). Depending on the industry, they may then add specific additional committees. For example, manufacturing company boards often have an OSHA safety committee. Chemical, oil and gas companies may have an environmental committee. Clearly, any corporation that faces the consumer, such as retail, financial services, or consumer packaged goods, ought to have a standing security and tech committee.

How to go about setting up this new board committee:

- Identify the knowledge and background this committee needs, and recruit new board members with appropriate security and technology expertise.
- The committee, just like the audit committee, should schedule regular meetings with the CFO and internal audit. It should also have regular meetings and reports from the chief information officer (CIO) and chief information security officer (CISO).
- Create a clear plan outlining the security needs and appropriate standards for your business sector. For example, in retail, the credit card PCI standard is applicable. What are the backup systems and service levels that are needed for your business, who has the right to audit the security system, what policies are in place in the event of a breach, how is sensitive data handled, destroyed and accessed? What best practices are recommended?
- Outside auditors perform independent audit oversight of company financials and control systems. So too a security and technology committee should have outside experts regularly come in to access and check the companies security practices. This is often call "ethical, white or gray hat" hacking.

While managers (and even the board) may groan about the potential expenses of such expertise, I have found the costs to be neglible. Boards are used to huge price tags for services—multimillion-dollar consulting fees from McKinsey, or corporate attorneys charging $1000 per hour. Yet I have found the very best cyber security experts typically top out at $350 per hour—a bargain for the value they provide.

Security and technology assets are critical to a company's value protection. The board needs to work with management and review their proposals on the appropriate budget needed for a robust security structure. If, as noted above, it is good value to invest in outside consulting to tell you what is wrong with your data security, an even better bargain is to invest in making your internal capability strong in the first place.

As part of your committee's ongoing security and technology work, there should be a regular review of the number of attacks and incidents that occur, and the effectiveness of the company's response plan. You need a documented recovery policy that identifies processes to inform customers, the general marketplace, and government authorities in the event of a breach. For example, the CIO and CISO could present their vendor selection decisions to the committee for review just as the board reviews other capital expenses on major enterprise resource planning software.

There are many resources that the board can look to for information on how to set up this new committee. For example, a government agency called the National Institute of Standards and Technology (NIST) publishes a well-accepted set of best practices on cyber security. The NACD (National Association of Corporate Directors) in 2014 prepared recommendations for boards in overseeing cybersecurity issues. It is crucial that the board require management to present their policies on cyber security. This is important for proper board oversight of management's plans on responding in the event of a breach. An oil or chemical company must have an emergency plan in the event of a spill. Likewise, the board should ask management what their plan is in the case of a security breach. Request that management write up their security practices and standards, and their protocol for responding to a security breach. The board should be able to identify the manager responsible by title, and in what time frame they are to respond to an intrusion. In the event of a cyber-breach, the board should schedule an update from the security committee on any forensic review. This update should identify what the investigation found, and should offer good documentation of any diligence done, and potential liability or reporting issues. For example, there is a Florida "information protection act" that could be violated if a breach impacts state residents. There might also be interstate legal conflicts, and there will be a need to notify the effected agencies.

There may well be other disclosure requirements. The company may need to disclose any data breach in SEC filings if the breach was material. There could even be disclosure requirements for an attempted breach. Your board might be surprised to find out that a court considers failure to disclose a cyber-attack as a "material omission," according to some interpretations of new SEC guidance on disclosure. Finally, in the annual review of your directors and officers (D&O) policy, your board should specifically consider additional insurance for liability related to security privacy and cyber risks. Ask your general counsel and CFO, when reviewing the annual D&O coverage, to see if any new provisions or indemnifications should be added to protect directors from a cyber liability exposure.

My personal boardroom experience on this can be instructive. I served as an outside director with the board of a direct-to-consumer software company a few years back, one that powered 40,000 websites. When we had a security breach, I asked management for a full forensic investigation. I wanted the board to know who had attacked us, and why, and what the short- and long-term implications would be. What steps would we be taking, and what new programs, policies, procedures would be required. I asked the chief information officer, the head of R&D, the CIO, and CFO to report quarterly to board. We held an emergency board call the day after the breach, another call a week later, and then a live present at the next board meeting.

Our board also told management we wanted someone from outside to make a forensic review. Management's initial response was that they could fix this themselves, but our board said no, we wanted an outside expert to help. One result of this close board follow-up was pretty good containment of the damage. The intrusion ended up costing the company less than we thought.

Shaping Your Cyber-Board: Board action items for cyber security.
Management needs to encourage the board to fully embrace cybersecurity as a governance oversight responsibility. The board needs information and training on cyber security issues so they are not seen as too complex and technical, outstripping the board's ability to exercise oversight. Cybersecurity is not the exclusive province of the CIO. The

board needs to know why and how it is expected to add oversight, and what that oversight might include.

The board should consider whether a change needs to be made in the way cybersecurity oversight is currently handled at the board level. Is there a need for a new security compliance committee?

The board may require new candidates with computer security background in the director nomination process. Would the "cyber savvy" of current directors give investors confidence?

Given the risk exposure involved, the board should work with the general counsel to determine the extent to which existing directors and officer's insurance coverage provides protection. Will you be protected if data breach-based legal actions assert personal liability against board members?

For the board to exercise effective oversight, they will need an understanding of what matters are properly reserved to the CIO, what matters require board awareness, and what matters require board/committee oversight, action, and/or approval.

Adapted from *The Corporate Board* January/February 2015.

The governance committee is the "judiciary branch" of the board. Directors need to be empowered to seek outside counsel when there are gray areas where the in-house general counsel may be conflicted, just as the audit committee uses outside advisors.

Defining the Governance Committee Role (Oversight of Legal Counsel)

Oversight of both inside and outside legal counsel is an important governance function.

The governance committee is responsible to the shareholders for oversight on how the corporation is governed. I suggest that this role includes responsibility for oversight of legal counsel.

The central question I am going to focus on is: Whose job is it to objectively advise the board when the company may be straying into the gray zone? If directors only rely on inside counsel, are they doing a thorough job in discharging their "duty of care" responsibilities as a fiduciary for the shareholders? Isn't relying only on inside counsel like relying only on the CFO and not checking with outside auditors?

I believe that inside counsel, when discharging their role of putting the most persuasive argument forward for the corporation, is no longer objective. The independent "checks and balances" function of the board can best be served by outside counsel. I posit that outside counsel should be the independent guidepost or resource to inform the board of conflicts, legal risks, and improper practices should any occur. The external counsel is analogous to outside auditors and ought to report to a committee of the directors. But which one?

"Judiciary Branch" of the Board

The logical choice is the governance committee. We need only look at the system of our United States government—the best in the world—to see an example of an optimal structure: the executive branch, the legislative branch, and the judicial branch. Applying that model to public corporation boards, the CEO chairman forms the executive branch; the audit committee, the legislative branch, as it reviews the corporation's spending and revenue recognition; and the governance committee is the judiciary branch that reviews the tone at the top and its adherence to proper business principles.

The governance committee is charged with safeguarding the soul of the corporation: Does the company have the proper code of business ethics and code of conduct? Has the company done compliance training so the employees understand the corporation's business mores? For example, are policies in place against sexual harassment? Is there a whistleblower escalation process published? Are policies on theft of intellectual property and competitive information understood? Does the company have an information security and document retention policy, and is it understood? Is it enforced?

Following are two real-life situations where inside counsel turned out not to have been an objective guidepost for the board of directors. These experiences have led me to conclude, as we define and upgrade our corporate governance in America, that we have missed a key element: the role of legal counsel, both internal and external.

These two anecdotes come from my experiences both as a director and as a confidante to other directors in their boardrooms. They underscore my point that we need checks and balances in the form of legal advice to augment our board, just as the audit committee gets advice from outside auditors.

A Questionable Cash-Crunch Solution

The first story is about a public company that decided to do a preferred convertible offering in response to a liquidity crunch. The in-house counsel supported the management's recommendation that some of the pension funds be used to purchase and support the offering. Corporation's preferred convertible. There was no outside counsel present at the board meetings.

The pension fund was overseen by an investment committee that was responsible for prudent, conservative asset allocation to insure that funds would be available to pay out decade's worth of pensions. However, the final "check and balance" of the pension fund was the company's board, as part of its fiduciary oversight responsibility. Thus the directors were all conflicted. Directors cannot abandon or subordinate their duty of care and duty of loyalty to the pension fund to the advantage of the corporation's liquidity needs.

My opinion is the internal counsel's client was the corporation: not the board, not the retired employees (whose pension monies were under discussion), and not the current employees. Since the in-house counsel's client was the corporation and the corporation's goal was to meet its liquidity needs, the counsel was conflicted, probably without even realizing it, and did not explain this conflict to the directors.

Fortunately, the directors themselves realized they were conflicted. Management's convertible purchase proposal using the pension fund did not pass. Had the directors supported management, the board and the company would have been vulnerable to a lawsuit that might have proved very damaging and difficult to defend.

Directors must have courage and a strong moral barometer of right and wrong. In this case, the directors could ask themselves, would they invest a significant percentage of their own pension monies in an aggressive preferred convertible offering of a company in a liquidity crisis?

As directors, we need to ask ourselves if we would be embarrassed to read about doing such a thing on the front page of the newspaper. If it just feels wrong, we must follow our own internal "cringe factor" reaction, and have the courage to disagree and say no.

Directors can no longer assume inside counsel is giving the board objective advice. External counsel serves as a better objective resource, in my opinion. Had external counsel been present at any of the board meetings, perhaps this purchase proposal would never have been raised.

However, just hiring external counsel is not enough. The board, and especially the governance committee, must oversee the workings of external counsel, as the second anecdote will illustrate.

A $750K Exercise in Futility

This is a story of a whistleblower incident gone overboard. A certain public company had not outsourced its payroll check issuing but rather did it in-house; the payroll department's check processing was not efficient. Human Resources had given the payroll department employees poor performance reviews; the group was concerned they would lose their jobs and the function would be outsourced. The payroll department manager was a particularly poor performing employee. He had received two previous poor performance reviews and was imminently going to be placed on probation as a step to his dismissal. This manager believed he had uncovered improper large double payments. He blew the whistle and had his attorney write a letter to the HR department.

The board was informed and created a special committee to investigate the whistleblower's allegation. This is where I feel the process went overboard. Separate, external board counsel was engaged to research this for the special committee. Outside auditors were engaged to do a complete review of the internal payroll and salary approval process as well as review and sign-off procedures.

In the end, this company's special board committee had spent $750,000 to investigate the whistleblower's allegation of inappropriate double payments. The very comprehensive (and costly) investigation proved there were no payroll improprieties. The error was easily traced. An employee had tried to stop a bonus check payment but the automated IT system went ahead and issued the bonus checks anyway. The company thought the human intervention had successfully stopped the bonus check issuance; it had not, unknown to Human Resources, which manually issued the two bonus checks. Hence the double payments.

The board probably should have truncated the investigation and negotiated a minimal exit package early in the investigation after it was concluded there were no improper chronic payroll shenanigans, and that the allegations were from an employee trying to avoid termination cloaked as a whistleblower. Directors must exercise their business judgment in discharging their duty of care and not passively create a decision void that in this unfortunate case was filled by legal counsel's zealous investigation.

The Value of Objectivity

I hope these two anecdotes illustrate that when things go wrong and legal issues arise in the company, the board needs to have objective legal advice. I contend we need to explicitly clarify the roles of inside counsel and external counsel as they relate to the board. I recommend that just as the Sarbanes-Oxley legislation has clarified and strengthened the audit committee relationship to hire external auditors, so too should the governance committee explicitly be responsible for oversight of legal topics and the company's code of conduct.

Clarify, Clarify, Clarify

In conclusion, we need to clarify the responsibility for legal oversight. This remains today a gray area in the boardroom that no one is discussing. We need to crisply assign oversight or we may inadvertently leave the corporation vulnerable to bad decisions made by management that could put the corporation and its assets in a potentially compromised position. The directors cannot abdicate their responsibility to make business judgments to their legal advisors, but without clearly identified independent legal advisors whose role is to advise the board, things can go astray. These stories illustrate the need for clarity of the legal role and for heightened oversight of that role.

Adapted from *Directors Monthly* February 2003.

CHAPTER 7: THE ART OF THE DEAL

Most large companies come up with one big innovation, then incrementally iterate. Creating an entrepreneurial environment means companies have to consciously create structures to foster innovation. However, most companies need to recognize they cannot continually and nimbly innovate, and so must acquire to stay competitive.

Will Entrepreneurship Survive?

A question and answer interview

Q: Are you surprised at the severity of the economic crisis and the speed at which it progressed, and where are we in the process of recovery?

Betsy Atkins: I did not expect this crisis to be as deep as it is, and I think it will follow the lines of the '20s, which was in the shape of a W. We went down, we've now gone up, and I think we'll go down again before we come up, because the debt that the government has taken on and some of the major programs they're looking at doing are going to enter the private sector. That is going to have a big impact. If health care is socialized, for instance, and 15 percent of our economy—which is the health care portion—is taken over by the government, that's going to hurt America's economy.

Q: Some feel the stimulus was needed at the time, but that real recovery is going to come back to the private sector via entrepreneurship and innovation. Do you agree, and are the incentives there to spur on that type of innovation?

B.A.: The concept of the government putting money into the economy could have been fine philosophically if they had put the money into small businesses. Seventy percent of the businesses in America are small- and medium-sized businesses, and if you'd given every one of them $1 million instead of all that money to GM, it would have really helped the economy. Historically, the government hasn't been successful in any of its enterprises. They're insolvent. Social security isn't solvent, the post office isn't solvent, Amtrak isn't solvent, and GM isn't solvent. I'm not a big believer that the government entering the private sector is helpful.

Q: With so much regulation today, are we stymieing entrepreneurship, and from a policy point of view, do things need to change to help drive innovation?

B.A.: Innovation by its nature often starts as a small business—it's entrepreneurial. The regulatory and tax burdens are going up, so that's not good for innovation. More importantly, this administration says it's going to take away capital gains, which is a key incentive. Everybody comes to America because this is the place where you can grab the "brass ring" and own it all if you work hard. The current government policy orientation is not supportive of that. That said, I believe the spirit of entrepreneurism has not died. Entrepreneurs in America will continue to innovate, and even in this somewhat unhelpful climate, we will still see innovation and new major breakthrough ideas.

Q: There is a debate about whether one can really teach entrepreneurship or whether you're born with that ability. Do you believe it can be taught?

B.A.: I believe you can teach the business of how to be an entrepreneur—how to write a business plan, how to identify a large and growing market, and how to identify an opportunity—but you can't teach somebody to come up with an idea. However, there are those who are entrepreneurial by nature and often can't monetize it. I've been lucky enough three times in my career to find entrepreneurial people with whom to start companies.

Q: As a company grows, can it remain innovative when it reaches a certain size and scale?

141

B.A.: Ninety-five percent of companies are lucky to have one great innovation, and after that, they incrementally iterate or add features and functions. Google is one great idea. Microsoft was one great innovation. There are a few exceptions like Apple; they created the Macintosh and then they came out with the iPod. Often when you're large, you are not structurally set up to innovate. If you want to create an environment that enables innovation, you must change the corporate structure and add a different structure, like a laboratory.

Q: Can the same person who initially creates and develops an idea lead that company after it has grown, and is it challenging for entrepreneurs to give it up when it's their baby?

B.A.: It is extraordinarily unusual to have an entrepreneur who can scale through the different growth stages. Most of the time, the entrepreneur may be good for the first $500 million. Companies stumble and you need a new leadership team, breaking through $1 billion, and again through $2 or $3 billion. You have to forward-hire a different skill set. You almost never have somebody who scales like Mr. Gates, Mr. Jobs, Mr. Ellison, or Mr. Greenberg. It is always difficult to have leadership transition, but the hardest one is for the founder to let go of the baby. That typically comes with some "fur flying" in the boardroom.

Q: Will you give a brief overview of your thinking around the lifecycle of companies and how they progress?

B.A.: I believe that, statistically, 40 percent of companies have disappeared in 20 years—they've gone out of business or they've gotten acquired; in 40 years, 60 percent are gone. So look at your company: where is it on that lifecycle? Cisco, for instance, is around 24 years old. It's middle-aged, so it acquires nimble innovators and tucks them in and puts those products through the existing distribution channel. The parent is not functionally set up to innovate, so it acquires innovation. Hewlett-Packard is around 45 years old; it's in the 40 percent of companies that make it beyond 40 years. Hewlett-Packard set up HP Labs to be able to innovate, because you can't try to foster innovation in the main company's R&D function; it can't happen, and it really shouldn't. Companies have an obligation to the shareholders to keep growing that main company through product add-ons, not through innovations, which by their nature would be different.

Q: When a company achieves a certain size and scale, do they need to acquire the innovation, or partner for it?

B.A.: You can innovate in a variety of ways— by product, by service, or by distribution channel. You can add a viral marketing component, a multi-level marketing component, a dealer, or a franchise; there are lots of distribution channel strategies that can be innovative. So it doesn't only have to be a product or service. That said, it's difficult for companies to change their business model, the way they go to market, or the way they create products. Companies are generally most effective at continuing to innovate through acquisition.

Q: When companies look to acquire, what are the key things they need to be thinking of to make sure they're going to be successful with the acquisition?

B.A.: Seventy-six percent of acquisitions fail, and that's a lot of wasted shareholder money. So if you're going to grow and innovate through acquisition, you have to structure an "integration team" and process, along with a series of methodologies to ensure you don't lose the entrepreneurs, at least for the first year, so you get the transfer of knowledge. A lot of the value may be in the entrepreneurs' heads as institutional knowledge. To maximize the acquisition you must get their product through your distribution channel quickly. You can't lose that window. You acquired this company because it was first and had a "time-to-market" advantage. Push it through your distribution channel and take advantage of that lead. You have to be organized in order to rapidly integrate an acquired company and get the products or services to market quickly. Initially keeping that acquired company intact helps. Companies may hurt an acquisition because they dismantle them too soon. Functionally dismembering a small, delicate 100- or 200-person organization and marrying it up into the big organization by functional area too soon, and you may lose value. Sometimes, you have to keep the acquired entity intact for 12 months to retain the value and to quickly bring its products or services to market.

Q: Are you concerned that the public perception of business is still very negative? Can more be done to get the message out about all the good things companies do?

B.A.: It troubles me that our press has decided that business leaders are villains. Seventy percent of all Americans work for small businesses, and only 30 percent are working for multibillion-dollar entities. While our press is busy saying all business leaders are bad, they're actually implicating their own realtor, dry cleaner, and cafe owner, as these are all the small businesses of America. It troubles me deeply that we're vilifying large business. Large businesses employ a lot of people, and they're the ones who can afford and do give the most back into the community. The press and the politicians have decided it's "populist" to go after Wall Street, which has actually created a huge number of jobs and wealth.

Q: Many have suggested that boards are too closely aligned to CEOs. Having been on boards for a long time, how have they evolved, and is the role of the board more in tune with what it should be?

B.A.: I've served on public company boards for over 20 years, and have seen quite a shift in the board's role. Twenty years ago, boards were more likely to concur with management's proposals rather than have a robust discussion. It's also likely management didn't see the board as a resource. Today, a board can be a competitive differentiator for a company. Boards are opening doors to facilitate business, using their functional backgrounds and expertise. They're more interactive with management in discussions about strategy, proposed acquisitions, or market shifts.

Most boards now have an annual off-site meeting, which is a two or three-day deep strategy dive. The board is involved as the company reviews its annual and long-term strategies and, importantly, reviewing the assumptions the strategy is predicated on. This level of exposure allows us to be more effective in our oversight. With the advent of Sarbanes-Oxley, there is a mandated executive session, which results in the board "processing as a team" and having deeper discussions about the company's opportunities.

Q: You have been involved with start-ups and can lead companies of all sizes, but also sit on boards and see things from the corporate side. Do you enjoy one aspect of it more than the other, or is it all fun for you?

B.A.: I look at board work as a "portfolio," like you would an investment portfolio. I serve large cap, value companies, mid-cap companies, and growth companies, and I sit on the boards of small companies. You learn from each and I cross-pollinate.

Q: What does it take to be a successful CEO today?

B.A.: A successful CEO is one who stays closely in touch with the customers in the marketplace. If you are not out with your customers in your market, you may miss the shifts and the competitive intrusions of the other companies, and you're unable to react. You get the best market intelligence when you sell something. If you get too far away from the buyer and what is important to them, you lose out. A good leader is somebody who has confidence in their views and is able to make informed decisions in a timely manner. If they make the wrong decision, they find out where they're off base, and refine that decision. Good leaders are thoughtful and analytical but also decisive. They are inspiring, have high integrity, and are courageous.

Q: You've been in the academic world and continue to speak to future leaders. What should they be trying to do early in their careers to grow and be successful in the corporate world?

B.A.: The one piece of advice I'd give to graduates is to distinguish yourself as the person who works the hardest, does what he says, and always follows through by reporting back, whether successful or not. If a new graduate cultivates those attributes, he or she will truly stand out.

Adapted from *Leaders* Volume 32, Number 4.

The board should ask management to prepare a plan to demonstrate how an acquisition will be integrated so the original value will not be lost. The company needs structure and processes to successfully integrate acquisitions. SAP's VP of Corporate Development (M&A) tells us we directors need to ask more probing questions on the pricing of the deal and if the underlying business case assumptions and numbers are too optimistic.

How Boards Should Deal With M&A

In serving on major company boards of directors over the years, I've found that evaluating merger-and-acquisition opportunities can be the most high stakes role a board plays--and also the most frustrating. Although some companies make regular acquisitions a part of their corporate strategy, for most such deals, especially major ones, are occasional, stressful events. Acquisitions inherently involve many uncertainties. Board actions and decisions get made on a hurry-up-and-wait basis. Decisions reached today are second-guessed for years to come. And often, no matter how diligently the board acts, there is an information mismatch between what the board needs to know to make the best decisions and what it can actually get from management and other sources.

I have seen most of the M&A process from a board's perspective. Seeking insight from the other side of the board table--the management representatives who actually work the deals and serve as a board's main resource, I've turned to one of the most experienced and thoughtful executives I've encountered on the subject, Arlen Shenkman. Arlen is vice president of corporate development for the global technology giant SAP. At SAP he has led, evaluated, executed, and integrated more than 35 acquisitions and strategic investments, with a total value of $8 billion. Before joining SAP, he was chief corporate counsel for IKON Office Solutions, and before that was a securities and M&A attorney.

I've found that SAP manages its acquisitions very well, including their corporate governance aspects. This surprises some people, who think of the big, fast-moving tech companies of Silicon Valley as the experts on doing good acquisitions. When SAP purchased my own company, ClearStandards, we had a number of suitors. SAP was faster, outmaneuvering them all, and I've been very impressed with its smooth, effective integration process. I've been in management or on boards in a number of industries, and I see SAP's acquisition process as a case study in best practice.

I sent Arlen a note with some of my thoughts on what boards should be hearing about M&A deals. Our subsequent exchange developed some good ideas on how boards and management view the deal making process—and how they can make it more effective. Here is our dialogue:

Betsy Atkins: I think boards just feel vulnerable in the deal making process. Most companies tend not to have a strong growth-through-acquisitions strategy in their corporate DNA. Deals can appear to the board as sudden reactive events that arrive on the agenda with tight deadlines, accompanied by too much information that has too little direct value. Sometimes I suspect management is in the same position too. Maybe an opportunity suddenly presented itself, or an investment banker called with this week's "deal of the decade." To the board, the CEO may seem to be struggling to make the case for how the deal will fit with the company's strategy.

I've found that even companies such as tech firms that build regular acquisitions into their growth strategies often don't handle the process as well as they could at the board level. For example, there can be data clutter. We get telephone books' worth of information when what we really need are a few key facts, like how fast and how well the company can be integrated, what unique benefit we will gain (technology, intellectual property, key people, access to a certain market?) and concise basic financial information.

That all can and should be boiled down into a short board summary, like the memos President Reagan used to expect from his staff. That not only gives the board the information it needs but also helps the management team, which can become so focused on making a deal work that they lose sight of why it's worthwhile. What is the strategic rationale? Do we gain any quickly grasped competitive edge?

I also think boards want to know how a particular deal fits in with an overall non-organic growth strategy, which might include acquisitions, investments and joint ventures. Suppose this does look like a good deal. Is it part of an ongoing effort to fill gaps in the current product line? Is there an overall template or model for an acquisition strategy for the next three years?

One M&A item that I think is very important is discussion of after-the-acquisition issues and integration challenges. Can you show me a brief timeline of the merger integration, showing key milestones and expected problems? If a goal of the deal is to get new key people, how will we deal with talent retention?

Finally, while looking into the future I think it's a good idea to update a board on experiences with past acquisitions, too. Sometimes when we on a board hear about all the synergies a new deal will bring the company, I have a sinking feeling that I've heard it before. Maybe it sounds too much like the acquisition we did a year or two ago. I like to see a good forensic examination of previous deals. What worked? What didn't? Why? Were the key numbers or goals met? Best of all, what lessons did we learn that will make the current deal better?

Arlen Shenkman: I really appreciate your insights on this topic, Betsy. From my experience, I've found that not all boards are as experienced at doing deals as you are. And like it or not, managers tend not to answer questions they're not asked. When it comes to mergers and acquisitions, the board should be asking: What are the key assets, skills, talent, markets or income streams that this acquisition can bring? What are the risks to our expected revenue and cost synergies, and who is responsible for them? I've seen cases in the past where a CEO or company counsel offered the board nothing more than a few clichés about "gaining synergies." Directors need to dig a little deeper into those "synergies."

Boards should be especially careful when it comes to judging the financial aspects of a deal. In my experience, I've found that directors just don't ask enough about pricing—whether the numbers make sense, why the proposed deal structure is better than the alternatives (joint ventures, investments, partnerships), revenue projections and why this is the best use of financial resources (or are we just taking money out of our left pocket and putting it into our right?).

And you're certainly right when it comes to unanswered questions on integration strategy. From the other side of things, I've found that too often the board doesn't hear about that because management itself doesn't know. All corporations, even those that rarely do acquisitions, should develop policies with both the board and management on how deals will be sourced, the factors to be weighed, and how they should fit into overall corporate strategy. The strategy should address not only acquisitions but also overall non-organic growth opportunities, including mergers, joint ventures, investments, and strategic partnerships. Then any potential deals that come to the board can be looked at in an existing framework.

B.A.: That's an excellent approach. Starting with a board-management acquisition strategy means potential deals are less likely to be sudden one-off opportunities (or something pitched by an investment bank). The board members then also know an idea has been fully vetted for a sound strategic case, integration strategy, pricing and so on before they ever become involved.

I've been very impressed with SAP's start-to-finish approach to M&A and wanted to discuss that with you. Can you tell me more about how it works?

A.S.: SAP's corporate governance has something to do with it. I think the German two-tier board model is good for the deal making process. There's a management-level board that knows how to develop good acquisitions, but it has to be able to justify them to the supervisory-level board.

At SAP, we have an investment council, a subgroup of our executive board, that works on M&A strategy. It's a global group, and it meets several times a year. Its makeup gives it a connection to the operating units of the business, and in that it differs from other boards I've been involved with. The group holds top-down and bottom-up reviews of acquisition strategy. For the top-down aspect, they examine where the board wants to go with acquisitions. For the bottom-up, they review what the people in the field at SAP's different units want to acquire. In each case, they examine priorities and the unique benefits of any potential deal.

Management is required to develop a summary document on any prospective deal, one or two pages of vital information. That sounds like your Reagan memo. The summary looks at items like the unique value proposition of the target, the business case, key risks and all the financial data for the target that we can access. The board makes clear to management that it needs a full set of facts so it can evaluate the deal.

B.A.: That sounds like a very effective approach. To sum up, what would you say are the key moves to make a board an effective player in making mergers work?

A.S.: First, get the board involved in setting an M&A strategy. Then evaluate deals according to that strategy as they come along. The surest way boards can get their questions on M&A answered is by building those questions into the process from the start. There are probably three key things to ask: How does the deal fit the business strategy? Are we paying the right price? And what are the key metrics we have to achieve to measure our success?

Second, the board should have the right blend of director experience to ask good, smart questions about potential deals. Boards are held to a much higher level of accountability today.

Finally, and going back to the initial board strategy process, build in a focus on post-acquisition integration and measurement. If the top managers can't give a board key measures on how well an acquisition went, whether the goals have been achieved, and what they learned in the process to help make the next deal more successful—then maybe the board should just say no.

Adapted from *Forbes.com Leadership* 1-5-2010.

You Can't Outsource Business Judgment

One of the most difficult decisions the board has to make is when and why to fire the CEO. Often times there are gray areas that have to be taken into consideration.

- The CEO may need to be removed due to performance.
- There could be issues of behavior questions, such as Mark Hurd.
- There could be questions of financial impropriety, like in the case of Ken Lay and Enron.

Often when these difficult situations come up, the board turns to outside advisors.

When bringing in outside advisors the board must be sure they do not abdicate their business judgment. It is important to remember that the board cannot abdicate it's business judgment responsibility. Only the board represents and is elected by the shareholders to be stewards on their behalf. The key, fundamental, and most important role of the board is to provide business judgment.

It is far too easy for a board to slide into the role of allowing the advisors to make the decision. The advisors are retained as part of a directors duty of care to obtain objective outside information before making a thoughtful decision providing insight into the situation, advice, and stress testing legal risks/alternative strategies, but in the end, the advisors need to be excused from the conversation. The external directors need to make an informed, objective, thoughtful business judgment on whether to remove the CEO.

In thinking about removing a CEO who is in the "gray area" and is being reviewed for either behavioral or financial impropriety (not performance), this is where the board needs to truly balance the scales of justice and remember they are not the morality police, they are fiduciaries and stewards for the shareholders, the employees, the customers, for the interests of the company long term.

The board always has to be held to the highest ethical and moral standard in their decision-making, but they cannot undervalue and fail to heavily weigh the importance of leadership continuity and potential destruction

151

of shareholder value in making a decision. Changing CEO's causes huge distraction on the leadership team and underperformance in the marketplace making the company more vulnerable to competition. Decisions should be made through the lens of how to do address, mitigate, and do appropriate damage control to shareholders, employees, and customers. It is imperative in making a business decision that there is a backup plan for leadership continuity.

This raises the topic of a coup d'état, Machiavelli in the board rooms, and conflicts of interest. My hypothesis is that a measurable percentage of the time, when CEO's are removed and a board member steps in, these actions are coup d'état's.

Perhaps we would see a better outcome for shareholders if all board members signed an agreement that none of the people on the board would step in as CEO, or become executive director in making this business decision. This would force the discipline of making sure there were internal successors which is a key role of the board. Also, it would eliminate the percentage of times when there truly is a coup d'état, and a CEO is changed because a board member has set their sights on that role.

Having a governance guideline that a board member will not step into the CEO role would be a healthy thing because with this guideline there would be no confusion about a potential conflict of interest and this clarity would lead to better decision-making.

In some board situations directors will face a gray area to be investigated. This is the essence of business judgment. How bad is the infraction? What is the level of action or punishment that is appropriate and consistent with all employees? Critically important consideration is: What is the disruption to the company? Does your company have somebody who can step in and do as well, or better when we remove the CEO? Will we destroy large amounts of shareholder value in removing the CEO? Could we make a decision to remove the CEO in an orderly transition allowing a ramp up time for a new person to come into office? These are the types of "King Solomon's Choice" decisions that board members should think through when making the hard decision of CEO removal.

First published in this volume.

What's Changed That All Boards Need To Consider In Selecting A Financial Advisor

We all know board directors are subject to the duties of care. The issues a director will face during certain sale or merger transactions are subject to additional so-called Revlon duties to ensure that reasonable efforts are made to secure the highest price available. The carrying out of these duties is subject to intense scrutiny. It is a virtual certainty that an M&A transaction of a publicly-listed company in the U.S. will ultimately lead to litigation focused on how the board conducted the process. So how do directors ensure they are getting the highest price available?

One of the most important things the board does when considering the sale of a company is selecting a financial advisor. Choosing a qualified, experienced financial advisor with relevant transaction capabilities who has knowledge of all the potential buyers will be one of the most important decisions you make.

It seems simple enough, boards and management need to select a financial advisor with relevant experience that can get the shareholders the highest price in a sale—so what has changed that makes this process more critical, and more difficult, than ever? In today's M&A environment, it is not enough to have industry knowledge and transaction experience.

The potential buyer universe has changed. The right financial advisor has to have a comprehensive understanding of the global cross-industry markets and have direct knowledge and access to a multitude of different buyer constituencies that have become increasingly new active buyers. To put this phenomenon in perspective, only 27% of U.S. based technology companies were sold to other U.S. based technology companies in the past few years, a huge shift in the breadth of the buyer universe since 2014. This expanding universe of buyers in technology has shifted the advisory selection from boutique advisors to full scale advisors with complete buyer reach access to maximize shareholder value.

In the past ten years, the M&A market for U.S.-based technology companies has experienced shifts in the composition of its most active buyers. The market has seen the rise of the new buyer-types:

153

- Foreign acquirors, especially China
- Cross-industry buyers
- Financial sponsors
- Institutional Investors becoming Active Shareholders

U.S. Tech M&A Market by Buyer Type

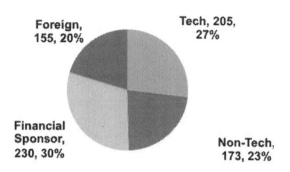

Foreign, 155, 20%

Tech, 205, 27%

Financial Sponsor, 230, 30%

Non-Tech, 173, 23%

These trends have become evident with Technology companies, with 73% of U.S. based tech sold to buyers who were either foreign, outside of the information technology industry or a financial sponsor since 2014.

Importantly, of the 27% of transactions where the buyer was ultimately a U.S. based technology company, a significant percentage had participation from foreign, non-technology or financial sponsor buyers in the process who bid but didn't win. The participation of these "non-traditional" buyers enhances the competitive tension of the process.

[*The trend is similar for larger technology transactions. Since 2015, there have been 96 technology transactions valued over $1 billion. Of those, only 29% were transactions where the buyer was a domestic technology company.*]

Five years ago when the majority of deals were "tech to tech", "domestic to domestic", "strategic to strategic", there were probably 6-8 great full-scale/full-reach advisors along with 8-10 great boutiques to consider for selling your company. Today, unless you are certain that your company doesn't appeal to the cross-industry or international or financial sponsor buyer, your smart choices are going to be fewer if you want to reach that broad buyer group and get the highest price consistent with your fiduciary duty.

Here are some trends that have impacted the M&A market in recent years and why now a boutique financial advisor may only address a narrow segment of potential buyers thus limiting the potential value in a sale process.

Foreign Buyers
In the past decade, inbound M&A activity of foreign companies buying U.S. companies has dramatically increased and is now a fifth of U.S. Tech buyers. Geographies such as China have increased their outbound M&A transaction volume. In the first 6 months of 2016 alone, there have been $28 billion China announced outbound M&A transactions (see chart below), including Ingram Micro's $6 billion sale to HNA Group's Tianjin Tianhai, which was the largest outbound acquisition by a Chinese company in the technology sector so far.

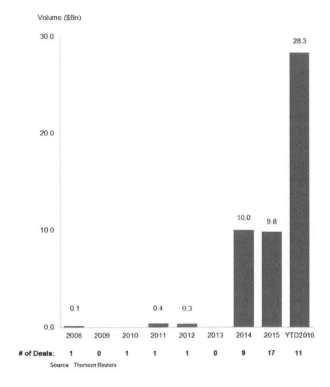

China Outbound M&A Exploding
2008—YTD2016, M&A Deal Volume and Number of Transactions

Volume ($Bn)

| # of Deals: | 1 | 0 | 1 | 1 | 1 | 0 | 9 | 17 | 11 |

Source Thomson Reuters

Additionally, tax inversions where targeted U.S. companies are re-domiciled abroad have been increasing common transaction structures attracting foreign buyers. Applied Materials' $9 billion merger with Tokyo-Electron (which was later terminated due to anti-trust concerns) was motivated in part by both companies' desire to lower corporate income taxes on future earnings through an inversion structure. The implication of these transactions is clear: an effective financial advisor must have a global network with knowledge and access to potential buyers who will emerge from other geographies. That gives you a number of great choices but they need to be from among the large, global firms that have bankers around the globe with access to and knowledge of these interested foreign buyers.

156

Cross-Industry Buyers

Increasingly buyers outside of your company's industry have emerged as competitive acquirors. In 2015 alone, there were $28.4 billion of cross industry technology acquisitions, vs. $10.8 billion in 2012. This is an amazing 263% increase in cross-industry buyer activity. Often it depends on your company's specific cross-industry appeal. A common theme has been cash-rich, mature buyers seeking new growth platforms to build on. Information technology provides lots of examples of nontraditional companies acquiring companies in technology such as Monsanto's purchase of The Climate Corporation, Verizon's purchase of AOL and more recently Yahoo, and Walmart's acquisition of Jet. For these acquisitions to succeed, the financial advisor needs the ability to advise the board to include these cross industry buyers in the sale process. More importantly, they need the relationships and knowledge to cultivate these new buyers who fall outside of tech. With 15 or so industries to cover, this leads us back to the larger firms that have access to the top buyers across industries, not just tech

Financial Sponsor Buyers

Financial sponsors, or private equity firms, have become increasingly active.

Sponsors M&A Activity Strong
2008—YTD2016, M&A Deal Volume and Number of Transactions

Volume ($ Bn)

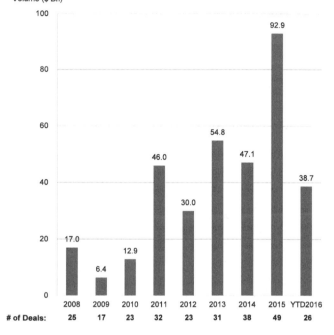

| # of Deals: | 25 | 17 | 23 | 32 | 23 | 31 | 38 | 49 | 26 |

To properly gauge the interest of financial sponsors and to advise you if and when you should invite financial sponsors into a sale process, your financial advisor needs to have close relationships with the relevant financial sponsors. Most importantly, have the knowledge to assess their financial capacity to compete against strategic buyers and know the maximum amounts they can aggressively pay. A key component of credibly determining the sponsors' wherewithal comes from the financial advisor's leverage lending expertise (both in the bank and bond markets) which are relied on to fund sponsor M&A transactions. Without real-time knowledge of the leveraged finance markets, your financial advisory will not be able to credibly determine the cost of financing that the sponsor relies on, and as a consequence, will not have the insights necessary to determine what price a financial sponsor could ultimately be able to pay. Several months ago, you would think ok, financial sponsors would pay 6.5x revenues and 69% premium for Cvent or 5.9x revenues and a 64% premium for Marketo which Vista Equity Partners did earlier this year. Having in depth knowledge of this market and the sponsor's financial capacity and desire is a critical component of the advice that financial advisors need to provide. We saw in the financial crisis of 2008 many of these financial sponsor-backed bids fell through, the consequences of misreading this market *(guessing based upon prior deals instead of being in the leveraged finance market trading securities every day and knowing what is possible)* can be devastating.

Activist Shareholders

Although not typically a buyer of companies, activist shareholders are another player now impacting M&A transactions. Activist investing is not only the domain of a core group of hedge funds anymore, even institutional investors are becoming increasingly engaged. Of the campaigns announced in the last 12 months alone, ~86 separate investors have targeted more than 160 companies. Of these campaigns, 69 have led to activist additions to the board of directors, 21 have led to proxy fights and 8 have resulted in sales of the target company. Many examples exist in technology of activists having direct involvement in situations which ultimately end in a sale of the company including my board, Polycom's, recently announced merger with Mitel which later evolved into a sale of Polycom to Siris Capital. Having a financial advisor who has an experienced activism defense team is important in preparing the board early in building and articulating the company's long-term plan for value creation and helping the management and board understand their strategic landscape and M&A scenarios.

If you think there is a chance that your company appeals to one or more global buyers, non-technology buyers, financial sponsors or that emerging activists will impact the advice and value you can get for your company, then you really need to consider the best full-scale/full-reach advisors with complete reach and access to all the increasing more common acquirer classes.

More M&A activity over the next year is likely due to continuing improvements in economic conditions, significant cash reserves and investor pressure for increasing shareholder returns. As M&A remains top of mind for directors. The factors that go into deciding the selection of your financial advisor should be carefully considered. Only an advisor with strong capabilities across all of the new emerging trends will enable you and your board to maximize value for your shareholders.

Adapted from *Business Insider* Nov 2016.

Miniver Press is a small independent publisher of lively and informative non-fiction books. We would be delighted to hear your questions or comments. And if you review this book on Amazon, we will be glad to give you one of our ebooks. Just contact editor@miniverpress.com